Indexing Specialties: Scholarly Books

EDITED BY MARGIE TOWERY
AND ENID L. ZAFRAN

AMERICAN
SOCIETY OF
INDEXERS

Second Printing, 2011

Indexing Specialties: Scholarly Books

ISBN 1-57387-236-9

Published by
Information Today, Inc.
143 Old Marlton Pike
Medford, NJ 08055

in association with

The American Society of Indexers, Inc.
10200 West 44th Avenue
Suite 304
Wheat Ridge, CO 80033

Printed in the United States of America

President and CEO: Thomas H. Hogan, Sr.
Editor-in-Chief and Publisher: John B. Bryans
Managing Editor: Amy Holmes
VP of Graphics and Production: M. Heide Dengler
Book Designer: Kara Mia Jalkowski
Cover Designer: Dana Kruse
Copy Editor: Pat Hadley-Miller
Proofreader: Mary Ainsworth
Indexer: Carolyn Sherayko

Contents

Contributors

John Bealle indexes scholarly books and specializes in arts and humanities subjects. Since 1991 he has been a journal indexer for the Modern Language Association. An active member of the American Society of Indexers, he has served as president of the Heartland Chapter (2004–2005). John is also a writer, and has published on subjects related to folk music. He lives in Cincinnati.

Nedalina (Dina) Dineva has been an indexer and indexing manager at Coughlin Indexing Services in Annapolis, Maryland, for nine years. A recipient of the 2000 Wilson Award, she specializes in the indexing of scholarly texts. Dina is especially attuned to foreign language issues since the primary language she is working in is in fact her third language.

Fred Leise is owner and principal of Contextual Analysis, LLC, providing consulting services in metadata and controlled vocabulary development, user testing, information architecture, and Web site indexing. Since 1995 he has worked as a freelance indexer specializing in scholarly works in the humanities. He currently serves on the board of directors of the American Society of Indexers and regularly presents workshops on indexing and controlled vocabularies. In indexing circles, he is well known for his First Rule of Indexing: "There are no rules. There are only contexts."

Kate Mertes is sole proprietor of Mertes Editorial Services (est. 1993), providing indexing, information retrieval, and editorial expertise for complex, challenging projects in law and the humanities. Kate took her BA in medieval studies, a PhD in medieval history, and a postdoctoral degree in theology, and after teaching at university level for several years, moved into publishing, including nine years as a managing editor of indexing for the Research Institute of America, a legal publishing company. She served on the board of the American Society of Indexers from 1998 to 2004 and as president of ASI in 2002–2003. She is currently vice-chair of the Washington, D.C. chapter of ASI. She is also a founding fellow of the Consortium of Indexing Professionals.

Mary Mortensen has been a freelance indexer since 1995 and has indexed almost 200 scholarly books, as well as many trade books and textbooks. She received her BA in French from Wartburg College and her MA in international studies from Johns Hopkins University. Prior to starting her indexing business, she worked as a data analyst and manager for large international banks in New York for 13 years. She now lives in Lawrence, Kansas.

Deborah Patton has been a freelance indexer since 1994. She majored in political science in college because the professor who taught the freshman year introductory course in political science was the brightest and most engaging of the entire faculty. Not much else became of political science in her life until she started her indexing business. Sending out marketing letters was a dreadful chore, but one of the early recipients was a respected Washington, D.C. think-tank—and they hired her. She and her husband live near Baltimore.

Jennifer Rushing-Schurr is a graduate of St. John's College in Annapolis, Maryland, which features an interdisciplinary curriculum based on selected Great Books. She was the final indexer for Ashgate Variorum's *Expanding World* series, a 33-volume, multilingual collection of essays on the European expansion. She is currently indexing the *Religion by Region* series, a study of religion and public life in the United States. She divides her time between Maryland and the Adirondacks.

Carolyn Sherayko has master's degrees in library science and English literature. She came to indexing in 1996 after 26 years as a librarian, so that she could have a portable profession. It wasn't until after her move to Lynchburg, Virginia, in 1998 with her husband that she started her full-time, freelance business. She specializes in indexing for university presses, primarily political science, history, and literature topics.

Margie Towery has been an indexer for more than a decade and was an editor for many years before that. Her BA and MA in history are from (what is now) the University of Illinois at Springfield. Margie's indexing focus is on scholarly books. She is the editor of *Indexing Specialties: History* (1998), the recipient of the 2002 Wilson Award, the indexer of the 15th edition of *The Chicago Manual of Style*, a member of ASI, a past president of the Heartland Chapter of ASI, and a founding fellow of the Consortium of Indexing Professionals.

Martin L. White has been an indexer since 1982. His formal education is in mathematics and philosophy, both of which he considers excellent preparation for indexing. He began his indexing career with Encyclopædia Britannica, working as an indexer, indexing supervisor, and in thesaurus development. The index for *Children's Britannica*, for which he was index supervisor, was a runner-up for the Wheatley Medal of the Society of Indexers (UK). He has been a freelance indexer since 1990, full-time since 1995. He specializes in scholarly books, but also indexes trade books, textbooks, and medical journals. His index for John Patrick Diggins's *The Promise of Pragmatism: Modernism and the Crisis of Knowledge and Authority* (University of Chicago Press, 1994) received the 1995 Wilson Award of the American Society of Indexers for Excellence in Indexing.

Enid L. Zafran has worked as an indexer for more than 25 years. She started in the field of legal publishing working for Banks-Baldwin Law Publishing Co., Prentice-Hall Law & Business, and the Bureau of National Affairs. She began her own indexing business, Indexing Partners, in 1990, and in addition to legal indexing, specializes in public policy, business, art, history, psychology, and education indexing. She has served on the board of the American Society of Indexers and as ASI President (2004–2005). She also edited two other ASI publications *Starting an Indexing Business* and *Indexing Specialties: Law*. Like Leise, Towery, and Mertes, she is a founding fellow of the Consortium of Indexing Professionals.

Introduction

Enid L. Zafran

For indexers, scholarly publishing represents one of the top areas for their businesses. In the 2004 survey that the American Society of Indexers conducted of its members, 62 percent of the respondents indicated that they worked on scholarly books. Only trade books ranked higher and not by very much. Although many of the general indexing guides offer advice applicable to the scholarly area, and many of the authors in this volume cite those texts by Nancy Mulvany and Hans Wellisch, there has never been one work devoted to this particular specialty. So when Margie Towery proposed the idea for this volume, I knew that it would greatly add to the literature available for professional indexers.

Margie assembled a group of contributors who bring many years of expertise to this endeavor. She has written a brilliant exposition on what constitutes quality in this complex type of indexing. When you read Margie's article, you will see that scholarly indexing is not for the faint of heart. It presents all sorts of challenges as you might well expect for a specialty that encompasses diverse subject matter, including niche areas within the humanities, social sciences, and physical sciences, commonly deals with abstruse concepts, and is not easy reading. Authors of scholarly books are typically academics who are writing about original research and presenting new findings or significant conclusions in their fields of work. These are not amusing books aimed at the general public—for the most part these books have specialized audiences that may be involved in an ongoing debate over a topic, and the author of one book may be picking up a thread from another. But in these books we have the progression of research, the furthering of human understanding, and sometimes the seed of an idea that will become significant in our culture. To make the ideas of these authors accessible gives real purpose to an index. Using such an index is more than looking up the recipe for tonight's dinner or finding the way to change the tire on a car (although each of those can be important in daily life). A scholarly index presents a researcher with a key to unlock the thinking of another colleague, and it requires an educated, sophisticated thinker to create such a tool.

Typically, the author of the scholarly book signs a publishing contract stipulating that he will provide an index. (For more about this, see the chapter by John

Bealle who describes his experience in self-indexing his book.) The contract does not often say how the author should go about finding an indexer or creating an index on his own. Sometimes a press has a list of indexers to recommend; sometimes the author does the index himself; and sometimes the author tries to find an indexer on his own (and in that case, we hope he uses the ASI Indexer Locator service). If the author contacts the indexer, then the indexer works for the author, although the press may provide guidelines and insist on certain style matters. This dual-client aspect presents another complication in this field. The indexer has to please the author as well as the publisher. Since the author may pay for the index directly, he has a lot of power; however, the editor at the press can refer more business to the indexer so she cannot be ignored. Given this situation, we hope that this volume can serve as a reference and guide—to show what others have done, why it was considered a good practice, and why another approach was rejected.

Frequently, academic writing involves looking at the works of foreign authors. The indexer confronts many foreign words liberally sprinkled throughout fields such as philosophy, history, art, music, and religion. Two of the contributors to this volume deal with the language issues—Dina Dineva and Jennifer Rushing-Schurr. A big breakthrough in my indexing life occurred when the publishers began sending PDF files. Now when I have to input a long foreign phrase or book title, I cut and paste it from the PDF file into my indexing software. Nevertheless, I am still confounded by the strange accents of Slavic languages or when a foreign term serves as a synonym for an English term in the same book. So I found Dina and Jennifer's advice of great applicability to my work.

Within the wide umbrella of scholarly publishing certain topics present unique challenges. Thus, this volume covers the areas of law, economics, public policy, philosophy, and music. In each instance, Margie Towery requested an article from a well-established subject specialist. Fred Leise has worked in the field of music for many years; Deborah Patton has developed a successful business in the Washington, D.C., area for indexing important public policy papers and books from such publishers as the World Bank and the Brookings Institution; Martin White has won renown for his indexing as the recipient of the Wilson Award in 1995 for a book on pragmatism (not an easy topic by any means!); Kate Mertes is a leading legal indexer with years of job experience for a law publisher before starting her own business with most of the major U.S. legal publishers as clients; and Mary Mortensen brings her background in banking to the field of economics.

And I had the best role of all—I got to edit these articles and to read them and benefit from their knowledge, expertise, and advice before everyone else. I learned a lot, even after indexing for more than 25 years! I recommend you place this book on a shelf you can reach, as you will return to these articles many times.

Chapter 1

Fantasia in C-Sharp Major: Indexing Books About Music

© 2005 Fred Leise

INTRODUCTION, ADAGIO MOLTO

What are my qualifications for helping you with the ins and outs of indexing books on music? I started playing the violin when I was 10 years old and, after playing in my junior and senior high school orchestras, entered the University of Maryland Department of Music as a violin performance major.

During my time in the music department, I studied music history, theory, and performance practice. I've composed. (Okay, it was for a class in counterpoint.) I studied choral conducting and have conducted professionally. I sang in the University of Maryland Chorus under such conductors as Antal Dorati, Julius Rudel, and the great Eugene Ormandy, as well as in the Chicago Symphony Chorus under Margaret Hillis. I even started graduate school for a master's degree in music history, but then sidetracked into my eventual career as an arts manager, working for a number of choruses, orchestras, and early music ensembles over the course of nearly 25 years.

As for my music indexing experiences, the first book I ever indexed was Dr. Samuel Floyd's *The Power of Black Music* (New York: Oxford University Press, 1995), now a classic in the field of black music studies. Since then, I've indexed a number of music books, including biographies, music criticism, and reference works (e.g., *The Reader's Guide to Music,* Chicago: Fitzroy Dearborn, 1999).

FIRST MOVEMENT, ALLEGRO: TERMINOLOGY

What makes indexing books in the field of music different from other scholarly works? Most important is the terminology. The terms used in writing about music essentially form a language different and apart from standard spoken English. Just as with other specialized vocabularies such as medicine and law, knowledge of music terminology is essential to properly index a music book. Hence, if you're interested in indexing music books but don't have a background in the field, you should consider taking a beginning music history course at your local community college or even taking instrument lessons (piano is a good place to start) to become familiar with the language of music.

Terminology can also be more or less familiar depending on the time period covered by the text. Books on medieval or Renaissance music will include more terms unfamiliar to the musically uneducated.

Examples of musical terminology you might encounter include:

Instruments:

- cembalo (Italian and German name for the harpsichord)
- cornett (wooden, mouth-vibrated instrument)
- Fender (brand of electric guitar)
- flugelhorn (valved brass instrument)
- oboe d'amore (alto of the oboe family)
- trumpet (modern brass instrument)
- vielle (string instrument of the 12th–13th centuries)
- viola da gamba (six-string instrument, played like the cello)
- Wagner tubas (special type of tuba required for Wagner operas)

Types of compositions/forms:

- arietta (small aria, usually in two-part form)
- call-and-response (back-and-forth interplay between two performers or between performer and audience)
- fantasia (free-form composition)
- ground (repeated bass melody)
- masque (16th- and 17th-century stage productions)
- mazurka (Polish national dance form)
- nocturne (Romantic character piece for piano)
- organum (earliest polyphonic music)
- plain chant (Gregorian chant; early monophonic vocal music)

- rag (early jazz form)
- sinfonia (baroque orchestral introductory piece)
- strophic song (song with repeated melody for all stanzas)
- tango (modern, syncopated Brazilian dance)
- tarantella (fast Neapolitan dance in 6/8 time)
- tone poems (instrumental works from the Romantic era, often program-based)

Tempo markings (often in Italian, French, or German):

- adagio (slow)
- allegretto (moderate)
- langsam (German: slowly)
- piu meno mosso (Italian: "more less motion," i.e., slower)
- piu molto (Italian: more; faster)
- ritardando (slowing down)
- tres lentement (French: very slow)

Musical styles:

- Ars Nova ("new art"; music of the 14th century)
- Ars Subtilior (rhythmically complex medieval music)
- baroque (music generally from 1600 to 1750)
- rococo (late baroque, highly ornamented style)

On top of the terminology itself is the fact that terms can also appear in many languages, depending on the nature of the text's source materials. Then there is the additional complication of historical terminology. Names associated with the violin family and its predecessors, for example, include:

- cellone (large violoncello)
- fiddle (generic term for bowed string instruments)
- geige (German for "violin")
- lira da braccio (Italian: "fiddle of the arm")

- lyra (earliest European fiddle)
- octobasse (giant double-bass)
- pochette (French for "pocket fiddle")
- quinton (18th-century, five-string French violin)
- rebec (medieval bowed stringed instrument)
- viola (alto of the violin family)
- violetta (16th-century, three-string instruments)
- violino (Italian for "violin")
- violino piccolo (small viol; also soprano violin)
- violon (French for "violin")
- violoncello (now commonly called "cello")
- violoncello piccolo (small cello)

Another class of terminology includes works that have music-specific meaning. You may know that "temperament" refers to a manner of thinking or reacting, but did you know that in music it refers to systems of tuning? Or that "cents" in music aren't coins, but a measurement of pitch differences?

If you're going to index books that include musical analysis, it's almost essential that you be able to read music, enabling you to follow the author's argument as set out in musical examples (which may in themselves require indexing).

SECOND MOVEMENT, ANDANTE: TYPES OF TEXTS

Music books you might encounter can be divided into five main groups. All of these types contain specific problems that will be discussed in more detail in succeeding sections of this chapter.

Biographies

These books deal with the life of a composer or performer and have all the usual difficulties of biographies, with the added complexity of dealing with musical terms and discussions of musical works.

If you decide to use the name of the composer as a main heading, you will probably want to collect discussions of his works under a single subheading:

Mendelssohn, Felix
    works
Schumann, Robert
    compositions

Either term is appropriate. In cases where the publisher is allowing you only one level of subheads (e.g., in a run-in style index), you can finesse this issue by using a heading of the form "[composer], compositions," for example: "Harrison, George, compositions." In cases where the book is devoted to one composer, you may simply want to use "works" or "compositions" as a main heading.

I find that in indexing biographies, I often use role-based subheadings to help collocate information about different aspects of a musician's life, for example:

Monk, Meredith
    as composer
    as performer

Such role-based subheadings may also be used to separate large masses of information into chronological or other suitable divisions. For example:

Bach, Johann Sebastian
    as cantor in Leipzig
    as capellmeister in Cöthen
    as capellmeister in Leipzig
    as chamber musician in Weimar
    as Collegium Musicum director in Leipzig

Hazel Bell's excellent book *Indexing Biographies and Other Stories of Human Lives* (London: Society of Indexers Occasional Papers on Indexing No. 1, 1992) provides important information on dealing with the vagaries of biographies and certainly applies to music biographies as well.

Music Histories

These scholarly texts deal with the cultural and historical background of the times in which the music was composed; such texts can deal with anything from the Middle Ages to the latest popular music trends. Such works can also discuss the history of a particular form (such as ragtime) or an instrument (such as the viola da gamba or the ondes martinon). Although not absolutely necessary, it is helpful to have general knowledge of the history or cultural context of the time period being discussed to guide you in your indexing decisions.

Theory and Criticism

Rather than focusing on the composer, these works discuss the compositions themselves, exploring how they were written. Books on music theory can be challenging, especially if they are dealing with the arcana of 12-tone composition or Schenkerian analysis. Again, the range of subjects can be extraordinary, challenging anyone's indexing skills. Terminology is often the most problematic area of such texts, so having a good music dictionary handy is important.

Philosophy of Music

Although rare, these interesting philosophy of music books discuss the why of music. What is music? How does it create meaning? A good example is Peter Kivey's *Music Alone: Philosophical Reflections on the Purely Musical Experience* (Ithaca: Cornell University Press, 1990). Books of this type are often best served by indexers with experience in philosophy, since that terminology will often be encountered more frequently in the text than musical terminology per se.

Reference Works

As with all subjects, reference works in music carry their own sets of difficulties, such as density of references and large format. You will want to clarify with the editor the expected level of indexing exhaustivity. Should you include every mention of every person or only significant discussions? What constitutes significant in this case, a few lines of discussion or a paragraph?

If there are limits placed on the indexing exhaustivity, be sure to indicate that in the headnote. One reference book index I recently worked on is prefaced as follows: "The index does not refer to trivial biographical, descriptive, or historical details that set the context for a discussion or that are mentioned for illustrative purposes only."

THIRD MOVEMENT, LENTO: TITLES OF WORKS

One of the more difficult and complex problems in music indexing concerns composition titles. *The Chicago Manual of Style* offers complicated editorial suggestions in dealing with composition titles (sec. 8.201–8.205 [15th ed.]). Certainly you should take a look at that source and see if it will be useful for you. Although this style manual provides important guidance, your author's usage may be idiosyncratic, so be alert to those differences.

Musical works can have one of two kinds of titles (occasionally both): "form" titles or "given" titles.

Form Titles

In the instance of form titles, the title of the work simply describes the form of the composition itself:

> concerto for piano (or piano concerto, depending on the context)
> quartet
> rhapsody
> symphony

In such cases, the title is usually given in roman font, capitalized:

> Beethoven, Ludwig van
> > Violin Concerto
>
> Bizet, Charles
> > Symphony in C

Qualifiers: Order Numbers

Most composers created many different works of a specific form. Joseph Haydn, for example, wrote more than 100 symphonies. Accordingly, usually appended to the form title is an order number that distinguishes one work from another.

> Haydn, Josef
> > First Symphony
> > Second Symphony
> > Ninety-Ninth Symphony

You might find these same works given a different title format depending on the author's usage:

> Beethoven, Ludwig van
> > Symphony No. 1
> > Symphony No. 2
> > Symphony No. 99

Note that in either case, you might want to arrange the works in numerical rather than alphabetical order.

Qualifiers: Opus Numbers

Form titles can have an "opus number" attached. Opus is the Latin word for "work" and simply means the order in which the work was published. Sometimes the opus number may be used alone to designate a work:

> Locatelli, Pietro Antonio
> > Opus 3

Often, both an order number and opus are included, in that order:

> Beethoven, Ludwig van
> > Symphony No. 1, Op. 21

If more than one work was published at the same time in a collection of similar works, then the situation is more complex. A work may have an order number, an opus number, and finally an opus order. For example:

Beethoven, Ludwig van
Piano Sonata No. 16, Op. 31, No. 1

That is, this work is Beethoven's 16th in the piano sonata form, his 31st publication, and the first of several piano sonatas published at the same time as Opus 31.

You may come across works that are designated by WoO. That is the abbreviation for the German "Werke ohne Opus" or "work without opus." These works are unpublished, usually from a composer's early years. Another possible abbreviation you might encounter is OP for "opus posthumous."

Qualifiers: Key Signatures

The key signature of a work is often appended to its form title as a distinguishing qualifier. Without going deeply into music theory, the key of a work indicates its "home note" on the scale: A, B, C, D, E, F, or G. In addition, the home key can be modified by the designation of sharp (#) or flat (b). Modern key signatures also come in two flavors, "major" and "minor."

You might see such key signature qualifiers as:

A Major
D Minor
G-flat (or Gb) Minor
C-sharp (or C#) Major

An outdated convention put "major" always in caps and "minor" always in lower case. While no longer common, you may find that your author uses that system.

The key signature usually follows the order number, but precedes the opus and opus number (if any):

Piano Sonata No. 29 in B-flat, Op. 106.

Qualifiers: Nicknames

Often, works may be given nicknames by the general public or by music critics:

Haydn, Joseph
"Drumroll" Symphony
"Farewell" Symphony

In formal texts, however, nicknames are appended to the form title and may appear in different places in titles with multiple qualifiers. Be consistent in your usage.

Piano Sonata No. 29 "Hammerklavier," in B-flat, Op. 106
Piano Sonata No. 29 in B-flat, Op. 106 "Hammerklavier"

Qualifiers: Catalog Designation

In the case of composers for whom many unpublished works are known, compositions are often cataloged by an individual scholar or organization. The published catalog then establishes an order of composition for all the composer's works whether they were originally published or not. Each work is usually designated by a catalog number.

The catalog designation for a specific work usually consists of an abbreviation of the catalog creator, plus the catalog number. The most frequently encountered catalog designations include:

> BWV: Bach Werke Verzeichnis (for J. S. Bach's works)
> K.: Köchel (for Mozart's works)

In the case of Domenico Scarlatti, there are three major catalogers of his works: Kirkpatrick (K), Longo (L) and Pestelli (P). So for Scarlatti's works you will find:

> Sonata in B-flat Major, K. 42
> Sonata in B-flat Major, P. 120
> Sonata in B-flat Major, L. S36

All of these listings refer to the same work. Usually an author will choose one of the catalogs and stick with those designations, so you shouldn't have to worry about conflicting catalog systems.

Given Titles

Composers may choose to give a work a distinctive title not connected with the work's form. In this case, the title is usually given in italics.

> Gershwin, George
>   *Rhapsody in Blue*
> Rachmaninoff, Sergei
>   *Isle of the Dead*

You may find occasions where the same work is known by a given title and a nickname, as with Mendelssohn's *The Hebrides* ("*Fingal's Cave*"). Determine the appropriate index entry from the author's usage and then create a cross-reference from the alternate name. Given titles may also be followed by any of the qualifiers discussed above for form titles.

Translated Titles

The author's usage should guide you as to whether to index by title in the original language or in translation. As with all such cases, you should include the alternate form in parentheses and add a cross-reference from the unused form of the title: "*German Requiem. See Deutches Requiem.*"

FOURTH MOVEMENT, CON MOTO: CLASSIFIED LISTS

Depending on the context, it is often appropriate in indexing music books to create classified lists of compositions. Such collocations are of great assistance to readers, who may not be familiar with the details of the subject matter under discussion, or if the text is exploring relatively uncharted historical territory such as women in early jazz ensembles.

You might want to include main headings by genres of works:

```
chamber music
     [title 1]
     [title 2]
     [title 3]
songs
     [title 1]
     [title 2]
     [title 3]
tone poems
     [title 1]
     [title 2]
     [title 3]
```

Or, if the text deals with many different composers, their names may be inserted as subheadings:

```
piano concertos
     Barber
     Beethoven
     Tchaikovsky
```

Or, depending on the context, individual works may appear as main headings:

```
Piano Concerto (Barber)
Violin Concerto No. 1 (Paganini)
```

It might also make sense to include classified lists of artists or performers, such as:

```
blues vocalists
     [name 1]
     [name 2]
```

instrumentalists
 [name 1]
 [name 2]
rappers
 [name 1]
 [name 2]
singers
 [name 1]
 [name 2]

Whatever the case, your guiding principles should be clarity, consistency, and ease of use for the reader.

FIFTH MOVEMENT, RONDO: PERSONAL NAMES

Names of composers can often be a source of confusion in indexing music books, as they may be in any type of text. In general, literary warrant should be your guide; that is, follow the author's usage. However, in some cases you may have to do your own research and look to context to guide you when determining the form of a name to use in the index. Is it:

Mendelssohn, Felix, *or*
Mendelssohn-Bartholdy, Felix

Mendelssohn, Fanny, *or*
Mendelssohn-Hensel, Fanny, *or*
Hensel, Fanny, *or*
Hensel, Fanny (Mendelssohn), *or*
Mendelssohn, Fanny (Hensel)

Wieck, Clara, *or*
Schumann, Clara

Beach, Amy, *or*
Beach, H. H. A., Mrs.

In some cases you may be clear on the name itself yet be unsure of its proper inversion.

de la Guerre, Elizabeth Claude Jacquet, *or*
Jacquet de la Guerre, Elizabeth Claude, *or*
Guerre, Elizabeth Claude Jacquet de la

Use an appropriate reference source (see below) to help determine the appropriate form of the name.

You'll also need to decide on how to treat nicknames; many musicians, especially those in jazz or rock have nicknames or pseudonyms. Do you index by well-known nickname or by unknown proper name?

> Morton, "Jelly Roll," *or*
> Morton, Ferdinand Joseph (Jelly Roll)

Especially with the peripatetic musicians of the Middle Ages or Renaissance, composers may be known by names in two or more languages:

> Lassus, Orlande de (French)
> Lasso, Orlando di (Italian)

Or worse yet:

> Landini, Francesco
> Landino, Franciscus
> Franciscus de Floentia, Magister
> Franciscus Cecus Horganista de Florentia, Magister
> Francesco delgli orghany
> Cechus de Florentia

Here again, a good reference book will help. You can also check the Library of Congress online catalog (http://catalog.loc.gov) for the form of the name they use. As with all indexing decisions, consistency is important, so once you decide how to handle a specific name problem, be sure to treat all names similarly, so that users' expectations are not confused.

In some cases, musicians may be known only by first name and city or town of origin, in which case they are indexed by the given name: Robert de Castel is indexed under "R." Guillaume de Machaut is indexed under "G." It would probably help readers in these cases to include a cross-reference:

> Machaut. *See* Guillaume de Machaut

FINALE, MAESTOSO: REFERENCE WORKS

This chapter closes with a discussion of musical reference works.

Print Sources

If you can buy only a single reference work for music, I suggest the *New Harvard Dictionary of Music* (Cambridge, MA: Belknap Press, 1986). This book is the classic in the field and will offer you concise meanings of a wide variety of musical terms. Or you might try the *Oxford Dictionary of Music* (New York: Oxford University Press, 1995). If you're interested in individuals specifically, then you probably want to buy the *Harvard Biographical Dictionary of Music* (Cambridge, MA: Belknap Press, 1996).

If you feel like splurging and are serious about indexing music, you might consider investing in the *New Grove Dictionary of Music and Musicians* (New York: Grove, 2001). It is the largest single-subject encyclopedia in the world and considered *the* definitive music reference source. The descendent of the original *Grove's Dictionary of Music,* this venerable, multivolume work has never been equaled in English and is rivaled only by the German *Musik in Geschichte und Gegenwart* (Munich: Deutscher Taschenbuch Verlag, 1980). Grove's latest edition was edited by Stanley Sadie and covers every conceivable topic from Greek music to forms to composers to performers. One important feature is a complete listing of compositions for many composers, which makes a handy reference guide to their works.

While previous editions of *New Grove* have had an English bias, its most recent edition has broadened its coverage of both music in the United States and the world, as well as of popular music in general.

The 29-volume, second edition of the *New Grove* was published in 2001 and is available in hardcover for the price of $4,850 (I did say "splurging"). It includes 29,000 signed articles by 5,700 different contributors. Grove also has published more specialized works, such as the *New Grove Dictionary of Jazz* (New York: Grove's Dictionaries, Inc., 2001) or the *New Grove Dictionary of Opera* (New York: Grove's Dictionaries, Inc., 1992), which are considerably less expensive. You can also sometimes find used paperback copies of the first edition of the *New Grove,* which was published in 1980.

Online Sources

The *New Grove* is also available online (www.grovemusic.com) on a subscription basis and is continually updated with the most recent articles available. Subscriptions (as of April 2, 2004) cost $30 for one month's use or $295 for an annual subscription.

The Glossarist site offers an annotated directory of online music glossaries and dictionaries (http://www.glossarist.com/glossaries/arts-culture/music/default.asp).

Yahoo! includes a guide to music dictionaries (http://dir.yahoo.com/Entertainment/Music/Reference/Dictionaries/).

CONCLUSION

Music, as with other fields of scholarly indexing, offers some unique problems and can often try the proficiency of even the most experienced indexer. But learning to speak music's language and meeting its indexing challenges offers the satisfaction of expanding your repertoire of indexing skills. A music index done well will leave you humming.

Chapter 2

Legal Indexing

© 2005 Kate Mertes

One of the biggest areas of scholarly indexing is law. The legal field is heavily published, and texts are often lengthy, complex documents requiring especially good finding aids. Legal indexes are often more strongly and obviously structured than other scholarly texts, with sectional breakdowns and an outline format, but the indexing process for legal books is not cut-and-dried. The process demands special skills. Indexers of scholarly works frequently find themselves asked to work on a legal project, or they may wish to break into the lucrative legal indexing market. This article provides an overview of the world of legal indexing for experienced scholarly indexers thinking about entering the legal field and for people with a legal background considering indexing as a career.

Legal indexing is not a good row to hoe for those unfamiliar with either indexing or the law. The learning curve is simply too steep. Legal texts often require deeply structured, complex indexes, and the subject matter is wide-ranging and complicated. Indexers familiar with the detailed subject analysis and creative structuring often required of academic texts will find law challenging but surmountable. Indexers with a background in history often find law indexing congenial, since much historical study demands familiarity with the law. Lawyers and paralegals clearly have the advantage as far as understanding the subject matter; but many good legal indexers do not have a formal legal background. In fact, lawyers sometimes have difficulty indexing law well because they are almost too familiar with the material; they may provide indexes useful to the specialist practitioner, but many law books are used by laypeople and students as well as practicing attorneys, thus requiring everyday as well as specialist terminological analysis. Nonlawyers do have to spend more time familiarizing themselves with the subject matter, however, distinguishing specialist from colloquial usage in particular.

TYPES OF LAW AND LAW BOOKS

The law covers all areas of life in which litigation may occur and in which questions of rights and privileges may arise—which means law is universal in the subject matter it addresses. As a result, many legal indexers specialize in particular areas of the law. The legal indexing market is broad enough that you can carve out a niche in, say, family, medical, and criminal law with a side interest in contracts, while avoiding such things as antitrust and securities law (with which you may be less comfortable). Other legal indexers are willing to take on pretty much any topic, but will tend to stick to a particular type of law book. And then there are those of us who will do pretty much anything for a challenge.

Although legal subject areas are essentially infinite, there are basically eight types of legal texts one may be asked to index:

1. College textbooks

2. Code books (statutes and regulations)

3. Case law

4. Treatises and monographs

5. Journals, newsletters, and other periodicals

6. Jurisdictionally mixed law

7. Supplemented texts

8. Encyclopedic texts

These categories are by no means mutually exclusive. A legal text on which I once worked, a 17-volume federal tax publication, was a supplemented encyclopedic presentation of the whole of federal tax law, with sections addressing various subject areas by statutory law, regulations, relevant case law, and commentary. Nevertheless, these types of legal texts all have their own idiosyncrasies, pitfalls, and pleasures.

College Textbooks or Casebooks

Legal compositions intended for law school students are often called casebooks because of their typical structure. Generally organized around a specific legal topic such as contracts or immigration law, casebooks present a set of legal resources for the student to analyze, professors hope, in the same sort of way a lawyer would approach a particular case. These resources will include reprints of articles, original treatises, material relating to specific cases illustrative of the subject matter, and a series of questions (and sometimes answers) about the topic and the related cases. Other law school texts will be more straightforward, monograph-type compositions.

Indexers often find casebooks quite hard to index. For one thing, the same information seems to keep being repeated time and again as the same topic is debated in analytic text, then the facts of the relevant cases, and then the questions. Moreover, the topic is not necessarily laid out in the organized, discursive method common to most scholarly works; instead, it is a kind of Platonic dialogue in which the student may go down a number of paths. This is because the book is designed to turn students into lawyers, and the whole legal methodology is dialectic (an insight for which I am grateful to Mauri Baggiano, "Indexing Casebooks," in Peter Kendrick and Enid L. Zafran, eds., *Indexing Specialties, Law* [2001]). The "questions" sections of casebooks are particularly confusing for the indexer in this regard.

To avoid getting bogged down in details, keep asking yourself, "Why is this case (or this question, or set of questions) here?" What is the legal point this case is being used to illustrate? About what topic are these questions meant to teach students? Case notes and decisions often contain a lot of subject matter that isn't relevant to the actual topic in question. A case in a section of a law book treating the issue of oral promises in contract law, for instance, might be about the sale of diseased avocado trees. The fact that avocado trees are at the absolute center of the case *is not relevant* as a legal point. The case is there to illustrate how the law treats an oral promise regarding, say, the quality of the goods provided adjunct to a contract for the sale of goods.

The audience is another important point to keep in mind regarding the indexing of textbooks. There are three potential sets of readers. The most obvious is the law school student. To what sort of student is this book aimed? Is it a general text for undergraduates in a prelaw course or for first-year law school students? Is it aimed at advanced students? The index is also there to serve professors using the casebook to teach. Frequently, professors use the index and other finding aids (such as tables of cases) to evaluate the book's contents when making the decision to adopt a book for their courses, making the index and end matter of special interest to publishers of legal textbooks. Moreover, college textbooks are widely available in libraries and may be used by the general public. So the indexer has to serve both neophytes with little or no legal background and professors with considerable experience in the field who are looking for specific teaching points.

Codes or Statutory Law and Regulations

Codes are publications of the text of actual laws or statutes, and/or the administrative regulations, written to put those statutes into practice. Some types of legal publications, called annotated codes, will include both statutory and regulatory text, followed by an analytical commentary, and organized by subject matter; that is not the kind of legal text we are discussing here. Codes are presentations of statutes and/or regulations without commentary and ordered by code number (which may or may not have much to do with organization by subject matter). Codes are generally state-specific or federal. Examples include the federal Internal Revenue Service Code and Bender's *Workers' Compensation Laws of California.*

The most difficult aspect of code indexing is that codifications have a very discrete construction. Code sections, often (but not always) quite short information bytes with descriptive (but not always accurate) titles, are almost always dependent on other sections for much of their sense and meaning. For instance, 8 Cal C Reg 30

("Cal C Reg" stands for "California Code of Regulations") on "QME Panel Requests" does not define either what a QME (qualified medical evaluator) or a QME panel is; the definitions are found in 8 Cal C Reg 1. The actual request form is in 8 Cal C Reg 30.1. Unfortunately, the separate regulations may or may not direct the user to these relevant sections, and the structure of the code sections may or may not organize the subject matter in a coherent fashion (the request form might just as well have been separated out at 8 Cal C Reg 75 with a bunch of other forms). It's the indexer's job to fill in many of these connections. When a specialized term like "QME" is used, the connections may be fairly obvious; but in many cases a word in general use may have a quite specific definition in the code. The indexer must be alert to such possibilities.

Besides the issue of separation of definitions from the things defined, codes tend to present other terminological problems. Specific laws may have a long, complex formal title, an acronym (which probably will not be used in the code book), an official short title (which may or may not be given in the code book), and a public, common-use title (which will almost certainly not be given in the code book). Users of the index may look up any of these four titles, and the indexer has to know, and provide, all of them. In addition, lawmakers often use idiosyncratic rather than common ("customer protection law" rather than "lemon law"), archaic ("dram shop" for liquor store), overgeneralized (boats as well as trucks and automobiles included in motor vehicles), or overly specific (motor vehicles defined only as automobiles, not including trucks) terms. And because codes develop and change over time, terminology may change (or fail to change), consistently or inconsistently. For instance, many states still use the term "handicapped" rather than "disabled" in statutory law; some states have changed terminology in some places but not others, due to the legal amendment process. The indexer needs to be aware of changes in terms and definitions, both as commonly used and as used in the statutes and regulations, in order to pull together scattered information.

Codes have many specialized topics, such as rulemaking, procedures, and notice requirements, and indexers generally have to make decisions (or follow established editorial procedures) about how and when to pick up these areas. It's common, for instance, not to have a main heading called "rulemaking authority," but to use this as a subheading under other more substantive subjects.

Another thing to look out for in code indexing is the tendency of code sections not to "fit" with the other sections around them, and for sections with specific titles to actually contain material in addition to what they are supposed to be about. Scholarly indexers are inclined to "follow the argument" of discursive texts, but due to the vagaries of lawmaking the structure and order of the codes may not, in fact, follow a logical pattern, nor are they necessarily structurally consistent. For instance, the pattern of a particular code may be to put material on notice requirements in relation to a specific subject matter in its own code section; but then one may suddenly find that, in material on liquor laws, notice requirements have been shoved in willy-nilly with the rulemaking material.

Should the indexer use code section numbers as index entries? In general it is wise to avoid using them. After all, code section numbers are easily looked up in the tables generally provided in legal texts or through the book's own structure. However, certain items (especially in federal law) are frequently known chiefly by their code section numbers: "401(k) plan" is familiar to nearly everybody. Code section number entries can be indexed all together alphabetically under "Section" and then numerically:

> COBRA coverage
> Code Section 401(k) plans
> Code Section 403(b) annuities
> Code Section 457 plans
> Control employees

or

> S corporations
> Section 401(k) plans
> Section 403(b) annuities
> Section 457 plans
> Secular trusts

My preference is to index them as if the initial number were spelled out and then numerically, so "401(k) plans" would be alphabetically listed as under "four(01)," followed by "457 plans" as "four(57):"

> Fortune 500 companies, employee benefit plans of
> 401(k) plans
> 403(b) annuities
> 457 plans
> Fraternization policies

All of these systems are common in legal texts, which seldom or never separate out number entries at the beginning of the index (unlike scientific texts). Whatever system you choose, it is important to be consistent, and if you are not consistent, to make consistent cross-references from one style to another. For instance, colloquially, people may be more likely to talk of "401(k) plans" but "Section 457 plans." If your editor wants you to alphabetize the former under "four" and the latter under "section," it's important to have a cross from "Section 401(k) plans" to "401(k) plans" (alphabetized as "four") and from "457 plans" (alphabetized as "four") to "Section 457 plans."

Finally, code books have an extremely wide audience. These books are routinely used by practitioners with a great deal of legal experience and familiarity with specialized vocabulary, but they are also widely consulted by the general public. The indexer must provide keywords for both audiences.

Case Law

The American and British legal systems are based on common law, and common law depends heavily on precedent—the decisions made by previous judges and juries in related cases. A great deal of the research done by attorneys in common law jurisdictions involves looking for cases that resemble their own, and many of their arguments will be based on the precedents set in those cases. So case law is commonly cited in nearly all types of law books an American indexer is likely to work on. We've already seen how important it is to law school texts. Treatises and monographs always quote from case decisions, and many code books contain annotations to cases in which the laws are quoted. There are also publications that consist solely of case notes and decisions, such as court reporters or administrative agency decisions.

The most important thing for the indexer to remember is *why* these cases are being quoted. They are there to illustrate a point of law, and it is that point of law that requires indexing—not the fact pattern or extraneous legal issues. If a text devoted to employee benefits, for instance, cites a case about the bankruptcy estate of a real estate agent whose estranged wife sued as a beneficiary of his 401(k) plan, what's crucial is the beneficiary rights of a separated spouse, not whether the defendant was a real estate agent or whether he was bankrupt. If five cases on a particular topic are cited, they should be indexed separately only so far as they may distinguish different points of law relevant to the main topic.

Having said this, in some cases, fact patterns may be significant to certain topics. This is perhaps especially true in workers' compensation cases, where certain professions, practices, and types of accident have seen the development of their own body of case law. Attorneys may look for any information about firefighters, policemen, truck drivers, and coal miners, for instance—these are all dangerous jobs with a great many cases arising. Slip-and-fall accidents, pneumoconiosis in miners, and accident-while-on-lunch-break cases are other examples of significant fact patterns that in some types of publication may require indexing. Once again, though, it is extremely important to place the indexable material in case law into the appropriate context. Is the point you want to index relevant to the section being indexed? One of my favorite workers' compensation cases involves a woman who swallowed a pen while trying to dislodge from her throat a piece of doughnut brought in by a coworker, which she'd consumed at a coffee break. The really significant piece of data in there— and the reason the case was being quoted in this section—was the involvement of a coworker in the choking incident: the poor coworker who'd tried to be a good guy by bringing in a treat. (In a later chapter, the same case was quoted in relation to accidents occurring while on a work break.)

Neophyte legal indexers are often confused as to whether to use the actual title of a case as an index entry. Generally, the book will have a separate table of cases (that the indexer or another person may be asked to compile or that may be done electronically), and the actual case names are not good index entries—remember, the aim is to index the relevant legal point of the case, not its every detail. (See Enid

L. Zafran, "On the Table: The Problems and Challenges of Legal Tabling," in Peter Kendrick and Enid L. Zafran, eds., *Indexing Specialties: Law* [2001], for a discussion of the production of tables of cases, code citations, etc.) But some cases are so generally well known (*Roe v. Wade,* for instance), or so central to the specific legal topic in question, that the case name is in fact a legitimate index entry, particularly as a subheading. The problem, then, is how to index it. While *Roe v. Wade* is always known by that name, many important law cases are often referred to by their second element. A case formally known as *Colony Inn v. Brown,* for instance, may generally be known, and referred to by the author, as the *Brown* decision. Either form is acceptable as an index entry, and if a cross-reference from one to the other can be included, that is a good thing. There may be an editorial preference for one form or the other, or you may choose to follow authorial usage.

Treatises and Monographs

Treatises and monographs—legal texts analyzing a particular subject area—will look very familiar to scholarly indexers. These texts are structured and written in the same sort of discursive style as scholarly texts and are indexed in much the same way. Legal treatises are distinctive, however, in three ways: They have clear text headings that nevertheless may be misleading; they contain case law and statutory and regulatory law material that may require special handling; and, in sheer size, they tower over standard scholarly texts.

A look at the tables of contents of legal treatises shows that they tend to be tightly organized, highly structured documents. This can be a real boon for the indexer. Legal writers of treatises and monographs tend to follow closely argued paths, with fewer of the digressions and side-arguments down which scholarly writers may traipse. Legal writing style also demands the use of text headings, which are a great guide to "chunking" the text into discrete parts. There are only a few problems with this: The author may drop important information into an apparently unrelated section or drop in a whole section that doesn't tie properly into the structure of the text, and the text headings are not always informative and may in fact be misleading.

Here's a typical table of contents section from a legal treatise, in this case *Bender's New York Practice Guide: Business and Commercial,* chapter one, section five:

> 1.05 Partnership
>   [1] Participation in Management
>   [2] Capital Formation
>   [a] Partner Contributions
>   [b] Loans
>   [c] Additional Capital Contributions
>   [3] Growth Potential
>   [a] General Partnership
>   [b] Limited Partnership

[4] Exposure to Liability
    [a] General Partnership
        [i] Joint and Several Liability
        [ii] Partner by Estoppel
        [iii] Liability of Incoming Partner
    [b] Limited Partnership

Now, at first glance this might seem like a very easy scheme to follow, and in some ways it is. In fact, you might almost be tempted to index it directly from the table of contents if you're strapped for time (something legal indexers have been known to do). Indeed, this particular publication is quite true to its structure. But many legal texts are not. For instance, section 1.05[1] contains a whole paragraph on comparisons of partnership vs. corporation participation in management styles. Since Section 1.06[1] is on "Corporate Participation in Management," the indexer needs to pick it up in the earlier section as well. Or the author might want to include a section on transfers of interest and be unsure where to put it; he or she might arbitrarily drop it in as 1.05[4][c], making it look like transfers of interest is a subtopic of exposure to liability, which it is not.

In other cases, the text headings themselves can be misleading. There may be material in the text beneath them that isn't covered topically by the text heading. In some publications, you may find a tendency toward "cutesy" headings that catch the reader's eye but that are not fully informative about the subject matter. And since many legal texts are frequently revised—some publications, like *Larson's Workers' Compensation* and *Corbin on Contracts* have been around for decades and are subject to multiple revisions—a text heading may continue to exist as a relict of a previous text but with a dubious relationship to the current text. There's no substitute for close reading of the document and a good knowledge of the subject matter.

Statutes, regulations, and case law present the same sorts of problems in treatises as in casebooks and codes, as presented above, and are subject to the same sorts of solutions. The final problem with legal treatises that scholarly indexers may find is their sheer size. Scholarly books average 250–400 pages. The average legal treatise is probably at least twice that, and some are far longer; of those already mentioned in this section, *Larson* is 17 volumes, *Corbin* is 12 volumes, and the *New York Practice Guide* is 5 volumes—and these are monographs. For legal indexers, an index of 5,000 entries or so is a small index, not a large one. This size element requires legal indexers to start making tough choices about what to index and what not to index, and to start building deep structure into the index, from the very first entry. While scholarly indexes have two and sometimes three levels of entry, legal indexes always have three and often four or more levels.

Journals, Newsletters, and Other Periodicals

Legal periodicals are indexed in much the same way as other scholarly journals, and nonlegal indexers wishing to break into the field often find them a congenial way of learning the trade. The main challenge in indexing these publications is in finding ways to handle the different elements included in legal journals. While scholarly periodicals generally consist of a series of short monographs, legal journals and newsletters tend to have a more varied makeup. Some articles cover legislative developments, others address regulatory changes and promulgations, and still others offer short summaries of recently passed laws or court case decisions. The journal's editor often will have established the appropriate indexing treatment for these sections, but indexers are sometimes called on to develop styles for them. The case sections may require a great deal more attention than their size and appearance indicate; the items have been chosen because of their importance as precedential case law. There may be 12 short case summaries on two pages of text, and each summary will require as much attention as a two-page news item. Legislative summaries, on the other hand, may not require much attention; they are more ephemeral items providing information about a bill's passage or progress through Congress rather than substantive material.

Jurisdictionally Mixed Law Materials

Many if not most law publications primarily deal with a specific jurisdiction: federal, state, or local law; international law; or the law of a single foreign country. In such cases, you may assume that if the general topic of the book is, say, federal law, you will not expect to have many entries under that topic. There will probably be a section called something like "state and local laws" with subheadings indicating correlations, distinctions, and interrelationships with federal law as well as some headings for specific states whose laws on a topic significantly vary from or strongly enforce federal requirements (many state minimum wage requirements, for instance, are higher than those given by federal law).

Some books, however, cross jurisdictions. A text on employment law, for instance, might discuss both the federal requirements and the individual requirements of each state. In such cases, it is extremely important to make clear to the reader what jurisdictions are being covered in which sections, in both the main headings and subheadings of an entry, and to do so consistently. For instance, if in such a book under a main heading "discrimination prohibitions" you pull out a subheading "disability discrimination" from a section discussing federal rules, you should make sure to create entries for the same topic in state sections. Depending on the structure of the book, this can be quite simple or quite complex. The trick is to treat the different jurisdictions as if they were "multiple metatopics" (to borrow a phrase from Do Mi Stauber's "Facing the Text" workshop and recently published book [2004]), that is, to treat the book as having more than one general subject area that requires specification in entries.

Supplemented and Revised Texts

Although scholarly indexers frequently work with textbook revisions, most academic books they work on are not repeatedly edited, updated, and republished. Exactly the opposite is true for legal texts, regardless of type: these texts are frequently revised and reissued, often over decades. The most frequently revised law texts are those issued as supplemented publications, usually in loose-leaf form, and meant to be revised on a yearly, quarterly, monthly, or even weekly basis. The number of pages to be revised in each issue may vary from as few as two or three to several hundred in each issue. Supplementation makes a lot of sense for legal topics that would quickly become outmoded by new cases and changes in statutes. But what effect does this have on the index?

Publishing houses that produce supplemented legal texts may have an editorial protocol for updating text, or it may be up to the indexer to figure out how to keep these indexes in order. The key to keeping a supplemented index current is good data management. One thing that makes legal texts easier to update is that they are usually referenced to a section number instead of a page. That section number will have a fixed relationship to the text to which it is assigned, rather than a flowing relationship dependent on space, type size, etc. So, if you know that only two sections in one chapter have actually been changed, you can ignore entries for the other sections—they won't be affected by the changes. If you are dealing with page numbers, however, you do have to isolate the changes in each chapter and look at every entry following the first change, in order to see how other existing entries are affected. If page numbers are used, they usually are by chapter, as 1–23, 2–12, and so on, where the first number indicates the chapter and the second is the page. I personally have never seen a supplemented legal text with continuous page numbers from the beginning to the end of the book. This is one area of work where the ability to compile a reverse index (that is, one sorted in page number order) in your software is a big help.

In communicating with the editor on such a project, be sure that he or she understands that you must see redlines (or revisions, or whatever you choose to call them), that is, pages showing the actual deletions, additions, and rearrangements of text that have been made for each issue. Some editors think you can make do with a comparison of the new and old pages, or simply the existing index entries and the new pages, and you can; but it costs the publisher more, because it takes much more time to locate the changes and figure out how they affect the text. (Some indexers bill this sort of work at an hourly rate, or significantly raise their page rates.) When working from a comparison of new and old pages, I sometimes use a technique called "topping and tailing"—comparing the first and last words on the page sets. If they are the same, the page is less likely to contain many big changes requiring an index revision.

Supplemented texts also require regular maintenance. Trying to do a quarter's worth of weekly revisions in one sitting can be confusing and fatiguing. It's easier, and the results are usually cleaner, if you revise the issues as the redlines arrive. In most cases, the index itself will be published on a delayed basis; revised index pages or the entire index will be issued, say, the first of every quarter for the previous quarter (or the revised index may only be issued once a year). Some publishers also provide current indexes compiled from recent additions to the main index entries. The mechanics of doing the index updates can be complex, and it's a good idea, if the editor has not already done so, for the indexer to work out and *write down* the protocols. That way the wheel does not have to be reinvented each time a revision is done, and the indexer is less likely to miss crucial steps in a complex procedure.

Time is also an enemy in grappling with supplemented texts. Errors inevitably creep in especially with split subject matter; no matter how strict your double-posting and cross-referencing rules, it's very easy to split the same concept between different terminologies over time. Legal terminology evolves quite quickly. What was once widely called the timely-mailed-as-timely-filed rule was, less than a year later, renamed the mailbox rule (which was, in fact, the common term for the same concept at an earlier date). A single missed relict entry for a now-deleted section can linger like a dodo bird. And over time, the whole aim or angle of a section may slowly change its tone without raising any red flags for the indexer. Supplemented texts require regular review and editing as a whole to keep them truly up-to-date.

Encyclopedic Texts

One thing that daunts most nonlegal indexers when facing legal publications is their sheer size. Legal texts can be vast, almost unwieldy documents that cover an awful lot of subject matter in exhausting detail, and this affects how the index is put together. While monographic material can stretch to many volumes, encyclopedic texts—covering multiple major topics over one or several major areas of law—are the most common type of very large legal text, and they present their own problems.

Encyclopedic texts, almost by definition, cover multiple metatopics. Most nonlegal texts have a single metatopic: for example, the Boer War, the relationship between music and the human body in the Middle Ages, or the 1964 World's Fair. All the entries in the index relate to this metatopic, so if it is used as a main entry at all, it likely will have very few subentries under it: "Boer War, dates of," for instance, or "World's Fair, defined." Some texts do contain more than one metatopic; a book called *A Comparison of the Artillery Techniques at Shiloh and the Battle of the Marne*, for instance, if it is structured in a particular way, might have two metatopics, Shiloh and the Marne, both with significant numbers of subheadings under them; and other main topics and subheads in the index might require significant qualifiers to indicate the metatopic to which they chiefly refer. But this is a relative rarity for scholarly texts. In contrast, legal documents frequently have multiple metatopics.

For instance, an encyclopedic legal text might cover the vast range of employment law. The term "nondiscrimination" will be used to cover both discrimination prohibitions against people with disabilities, by race, age, and sex, and so on, as well as for the nondiscrimination rules required for employee benefit plans to be qualified for tax-exempt status, a totally different subject. A topic "reportable events" might refer either to changes in an employee plan participant's status or to changes in employer plans themselves. State and federal laws may be discussed, and these different jurisdictions may need to be indicated. The indexer must make sure these topics are all clearly distinguished. The complexity of terminological relationships in an encyclopedic text usually demands deep structure, that is, more than one level of subheading.

Deep structure is also required simply by the amount of information presented in a large text. Discussions of a small topic may range over many pages and section numbers, requiring intensive breakdowns. Legal indexers are seldom able to restrict their work to fewer than three levels, and they spend a great deal of time finding creative ways to "break out" subsets of main entries and give them their own main headings. Multiple metatopics in and of themselves may add a whole level to the entire index.

Because legal texts are often very long, their indexes are often very large, and their arrays (a main heading together with all its subheadings) are proportionately longer as well, with multiple columns over several pages. As a result, the wording of subheadings becomes very important. Users can't simply scan all the subentries under a main topic to find what they want; they have to be able to locate it alphabetically or chronologically. Legal indexes seldom allow prepositions and "small words" as initial subheading terms, since they get in the way of quick scanning, and reverses are very common. The indexers spend a lot of time formulating strong subheadings and are likely to list the same topic multiple times under the same main heading to cover all the bases:

> Fiduciaries
>> bonding requirements of supervisors handling plan funds, 3.04
>> supervisors handling plan funds, bonding requirements for, 3.04

These two entries might be separated by 20 or more other subheads, so it's important to post both.

One of the blessings of legal indexing is that the final page count of the index seldom emerges as an issue, and you don't have to worry about cutting the index to fit a predetermined space. However, the size of indexes for encyclopedic texts does introduce data management issues. It can take half a day simply to spell-check one of these monsters. A proper edit can take a week—or two. You must make sure to allow plenty of time for the polishing of the final product.

LAW ONLINE

Everything about legal indexing that's been discussed up until now applies equally to all media: print materials, CD-ROMs, and Web sites. But online indexing of legal materials has a few special quirks. Legal publishers have a rather staid public image, but they were one of the first industries to take advantage of electronic media to manage and access large volumes of information, starting way back in the 1980s (when dinosaurs roamed the earth). As a result, many legal publishers had to develop proprietary systems, since there were few commercial software packages available to handle the size and complexity of legal materials, and many of those are still in place, in whole or in part. So the first thing the indexer should do, when asked to work on an online legal site, is to find out its history and locate any documentation or manuals available. Due to their history, these sites often have Byzantine ways of doing things and a fixed and not necessarily intuitive way of creating entries.

The online legal indexer will probably not have to worry about embedding, but nevertheless locator issues may arise. Since electronic legal indexes are often large, complex, and frequently updated, embedding doesn't usually work for these products—it takes too long, the updates are too frequent and close together to turn the files over to an indexer, and maintaining structure in an embedded product is difficult enough in a simple index, let alone a complex one. Moreover, most legal publishers large enough to maintain such a site usually have good information technology professionals working for them. Commonly, the indexer is asked to use an already-placed anchor as the locator, and the IT department runs a program that turns all page locators in the index into hypertext links. This usually works quite smoothly. However, the locators themselves are often problematic. They are not usually designed with ease of use in mind (since they are seldom seen or used in the "live" electronic environment), so they are often a confusing jumble of letters, numbers, and symbols that take a long time to enter and are fatally easy to mistype. Further, electronic legal texts often represent only the latest rendition of a particular publication, involving both print and CD-ROM versions (not to mention condensed and expanded versions), and these versions may all employ different types of locators. The indexer may be asked to maintain a single index for all these versions, with different sets of locators. This can be kind of fun if you like puzzles—or a real problem to maintain. For instance, the index database may contain entries like this:

Bankruptcy
pension plan distributions, effect on, {45.673}[45.6(a)(12)(c)]

in which the number in curly brackets represents the locator for the electronic product, and the number in square brackets the locator for the paper product. The indexer is probably the person who gets the job of stripping out the unneeded set of locators and setting the (usually different) set of general publishing rubrics for each publication of the different indexes.

The role of the indexer in online publications is expanding. Indexers have become involved in the information architecture of legal sites and in developing the taxonomical structures and search features whereby users "drill down" through a Web site to find the information they need. Since online legal material is so complex and so lengthy, users are always going to need very good finding aids—and indexers are some of the best people to construct these, whatever form they take.

GETTING LEGAL INDEXING WORK

Okay, so nothing I've said has put you off, and you've decided you'd like to try legal indexing. How does someone break into the field? First, build on the skills you have in related fields. Medical indexers often have to deal with legal issues; you may be able to take on a legal book dealing primarily with medical issues (such as malpractice). And don't forget your life skills; if you spent a few years as a paralegal, went to law school, or have been a practitioner, utilize it.

Sometimes it's whom you know. Find a mentor. Talk to editors and other indexers who know your work. They may feel comfortable starting you off on a small project without tough time constraints. Small projects generally are good for beginning indexers and for people entering a new subject area. Unlike other fields, law textbooks are not generally a good starting point for beginners. As I've mentioned above, casebooks can be quite confusing to index even for experienced people. But there are many texts aimed at nonpractitioners (human resources law is one obvious area where many of the users will not be lawyers), and these are good projects for people new to indexing or law.

Alternatively, working with another, more experienced indexer or editor on a large project can be a good way to break into legal indexing. A project manager overseeing the indexing of a large publication may need someone who can do specifically defined tasks or index prescribed areas. If you are quick, reliable, and accurate within the limits of your beginner's knowledge, you can provide assistance, gain experience, and come off as a good hiring prospect for future work.

SEVEN FEATURES OF LEGAL INDEXING

To summarize, there are seven features of legal indexing that both novices and experienced persons need to keep in mind.

Size matters: Legal indexes are frequently large, complex, multivolume works; and size is a complicating factor in indexing. Size affects depth of structure and often leads to multiple metatopics and to geometric as well as mathematical increases in the editing process.

Multiple metatopics: A lot of legal books cover more than one major field. Identifying the metatopics and figuring out a scheme for accommodating them is a major initial step in setting up the structure of a legal index.

Deep structure: Size and multiple metatopics often mean that legal indexes require a very deep structure to cover the subject matter adequately. But since deep structure can be very confusing, it's important to plan the index architecture as clearly as possible and to find ways to "de-nest" complex entries.

Time goes by, and so does the index: Many, if not most, legal indexes are frequently revised as the law changes and material is added, subtracted, or substantially rewritten. Indexers dealing with supplementation must figure out strategies for keeping their work accurate and be prepared to periodically reindex texts that have undergone substantial changes. Even the best-planned indexes and updating schemes can begin to collapse under the weight of frequent changes; minor mistakes and missed alterations pile up, and sometimes the whole emphasis of the text changes subtly over time so that the index structure no longer reflects the text properly.

Text structures and topic headings: Legal texts tend to be highly structured, with lots of topical headings. Don't make the mistake of thinking that you can index the text from the outline. Important information can lurk in unexpected places; topic headings can be misleading. There's simply no substitute for reading the text. With many big legal texts, usually with multiple authors, the indexer may be the only person who has actually read the whole thing (kind of a scary thought).

Where's the beef? Especially when it comes to case law, the indexer of legal texts always has to be thinking, "Where's the beef?" What is the real point of a particular case or set of circumstances? How does it relate to the main topic? Just because the case is about, say, avocado trees, doesn't mean it's there because avocado trees are important. It's there to illustrate a point of law. Many people think of law as a very concrete, straightforward topic, but legal writers are often curiously allusive, and the indexer must discern the real topic and capture it for reference.

Location, location, location: In many legal indexes, locators are not page numbers, but section numbers. Using section numbers makes it much easier to maintain indexes for supplemented texts and allows the indexer to work in advance of final pages with more ease. But section numbering also "chunks" the text and can affect the final structure. As with use of topic headings, indexers need to watch that use of section numbers doesn't just lead to a regurgitation of the text outline in alphabetical form. The section numbers can offer great help in discerning relationships between topics, but they can also be incomplete or inaccurate.

But the final point is: *law is fun.* Law is a blast. It's not boring or dry. Law is every quirk in human behavior. Law is life. Give it a try.

REFERENCES
Print

Ballentine's Law Dictionary. 1969. Rochester, NY: Lawyers Cooperative Publishing. [All legal indexers should have a decent law dictionary to hand. I'm using this rather ancient edition of *Ballentine's,* but *Black's* and several others are just as good. While new terms are added and definitions are revised, law dictionaries don't change much over time; I bought this version new in 1990.]

Brenner, Diane, and Marilyn Rowland, eds. 2000. *Beyond Book Indexing: How to Get Started in Web Indexing, Embedded Indexing, and Other Computer-Based Media.* Medford, NJ: Information Today and American Society of Indexers.

Brief Entry: A Newsletter for Law Indexers. [This was an international legal indexing journal. It only ran to a few issues and is now defunct, but several law libraries subscribed to it "Indexing for CD-Rom Products," "Plain Legal Language," "Wellisch on Legal Texts," "Indexing Textbooks for Secondary and Tertiary Level Students of Law," "Surfin' the Law (Using the Internet for Legal Research in the U.K.)," and "The Computer Teaching Initiative Law Seminar."]

Kendrick, Peter, and Enid L. Zafran, eds. 2001. *Indexing Specialties: Law.* Medford, NJ: Information Today and American Society of Indexers. [Contains many useful and highly specialized articles about law indexing.]

Managing Large Indexing Projects: Papers from the 24th Annual Meeting of the American Society of Indexers, San Antonio, Texas, May 23, 1992. 1992. Port Aransas, TX: American Society of Indexers. [Full of excellent articles about handling big projects, legal or otherwise.]

Moys, Elizabeth M. 1993. *Indexing Legal Materials.* London: Society of Indexers Occasional Papers on Indexing, no. 2. [Nuanced toward British law, but with much of relevance to American indexers.]

Mulvany, Nancy C. 1994. *Indexing Books.* Chicago: University of Chicago Press. [The best general book about the art and science of indexing.]

Stauber, Do Mi. 2004. *Facing the Text: Content and Structure in Book Indexing.* Eugene, OR: Cedar Row Press. [A superb guide for book indexing, with many practical examples.]

Web Sites

You may want to look at the Web sites for BNA (www.bna.com), Lexis (www.lexis.com), and Westlaw (www.westlaw.com), all of which have extensive finding aids. These are private sites that charge for full access, but usually allow partial or trial use of the site. Federal government sites such as the Department of Labor (www.dol.gov), which are free, will also give you some ideas about online indexing. State governments also have sites on which they sometimes include indexes to their state legislative sessions, statutes, and/or administrative rules.

Chapter 3

Political Science and Public Affairs Indexing; or, What's Harry Truman's Middle Name?

© 2005 Deborah Patton

This chapter provides an overview of qualifications for political science and public affairs indexing, reference tools, indexable material, and index styles.

QUALIFICATIONS

Here's how I found out I had qualifications for this subject area: I didn't purposefully set out to develop expertise in political science and public affairs. When it came time to declare my major in college, I recall quite vividly feeling that it didn't really matter and that I needed to just choose one. I was getting a liberal education. I chose to major in political science because at least one professor was intellectually stimulating. He thought outside the box. My major had no practical application (or so I thought) since I primarily read political philosophy to get my degree. I got it done. I graduated. And that was that—I didn't know what I was vocationally suited for. I tried several different vocations but none was satisfying or generated enough income to make it worthwhile until I stumbled upon indexing.

I couldn't avoid putting "major: political science" on my résumé. One of my first indexing jobs came as a result of that major. Astounding. I'm hard pressed to say what other qualifications will get you indexing work in this area. This worked for me. I would think a college degree and a genuine interest in the subject matter would be essential.

RESOURCES

That first job came with a style sheet and expectations that I would have certain references handy. First and foremost was a current world almanac. Since indexing

31

has become my vocation, I buy an almanac or two each year and I don't discard the old one. That first client expected that I'd provide complete names in the index whether or not the author had used a complete name. That meant looking for senators' and representatives' names in an official roster. Usually the almanacs supply the necessary roster. This first project also meant buying my own biographical dictionary. I use two because each dictionary has a different focus. *Merriam Webster's Biographical Dictionary* (1995 ed.) has "essential information on more than 30,000 men and women of the past." That means that if these people are alive today, they aren't in this one. For the living or recently living, I turn to the *Cambridge Biographical Encyclopedia* (1994 ed.). There's also the *Cambridge Biographical Dictionary* (1996), which I don't have but will likely add to my collection at some point since it includes living people. It's amazing how many times authors use incomplete names. While it's a basic rule of all indexing to follow the language of the text, complete names in the index can offer clarification when the text has been casual about who's who.

I would say with political science and public affairs indexing you'll find yourself wrestling with more names of people than of places. Ignatius Kutu Acheampong led a coup in Ghana in 1972 and then led the country for a number of years. He's not in any of my biographical dictionaries or the recent almanac. Fortunately, the author referred to him by surname, Acheampong, a few paragraphs after first naming him, which showed me how to invert his name to place him in the index.

When the author doesn't provide a clue such as that one did, I look for name inversions in the references section. I'm not always sure, culture to culture, which names are inverted and which are not. To be sure, *The Chicago Manual of Style* and Nancy Mulvany's *Indexing Books* have tips, but they don't cover every country. When the text mentions an individual after the initial introduction, I am often able to use that as the surname. But when that name differs from what's in the references section (when it's listed there), then I ask the editor which way to go or whether to double-post. Lots of people ask name inversion questions on Index-L, an indexing listserv, but it's really the author and editor who make those decisions.

When Mobutu is referred to, is it Joseph Désiré Mobutu or Mobutu Sese Seko? That's the same person who changed his name. The obvious choices here are to double-post or use a cross-reference. The editor or author may have a preference. I always ask about the shah of Iran—I have been directed to use just "shah of Iran" but other times have been directed to use "Pahlavi, Reza Shah" (as in Chambers) or "Reza Shah Pahlavi" (as in Webster's). We just cannot make assumptions about names.

As an undergraduate, I served an internship on Capitol Hill and became familiar with the GPO Style Manual. I haven't chosen to get one for an indexing reference, although I know others who index in this subject area use it. It's available online at www.gpoaccess.gov/stylemanual/browse.html, through the Government Printing Office. This source is dated but it's still a starting point for finding a more recent edition.

CONSISTENCY

I often find spelling or wording discrepancies. For example:

United Nations Program for Reconstruction and Development, 66
United Nations Programme for Reconstruction and Development, 80

Often the editor doesn't know something is spelled two different ways in the same book.

I also find inconsistencies in congressional committees and government departments. Narrative writing requires variation so the reader doesn't get bored. Indexing requires consistency so readers can depend on the indexing scheme. We see all kinds of variations in the names of congressional committees. If you decide to use "House Judiciary Committee," then by all means don't also use "House Committee on Government Operations." The second form may be correct but it isn't consistent with the first one. It's important to make the index use parallel structures to scan well, so violating the official title to make it consistent within the index is okay. I'd change the second example to "House Government Operations Committee." That turns "Committee" into filler instead of the key word on which alphabetical order depends.

STRUCTURE

There's also the question of "U.S. Department of Justice" and similar government organizations. If the book is about more than one country's justice department, then this form is important. If the book is about the United States federal and state governments, then this form is important. But if the book is about politics at the federal level or government operations at the federal level, then "Justice Department" will do. Sometimes I find myself putting in "Justice, Department of" but obviously that doesn't make for a tight index. Nonetheless, it's more formal and can be appropriate if the author's text is more formal. If I need to be formal but am really crunched for space, I abbreviate: "Justice, Dept. of." I sometimes also need to deal with the acronym DOJ—often I don't have enough space to double-post acronyms, so I put it in parentheses after the term like this: "Justice, Dept. of (DOJ)."

What I cannot tolerate is a mixture of terms under United States with cross-references to terms under U.S. An editor sent me a previous index to a book I was indexing for a subsequent edition that had the entry: United States, *see also* U.S. entries. None of the terms that were listed under U.S. were officially named U.S.—those were all abbreviations for United States. Choose one and use it for all the entities.

A similar problem arises from organizations affiliated with the United Nations. So many of these organizations have subordinate organizations that it can be a real tangle. I start out by making the organization subheads of "United Nations." When the subordinate organizations begin to have a lot of mentions, then we need sub-subheads; however, most of these indexes are required to have only two levels of analysis.

That's when the subordinate organizations become main headings. The United Nations and its affiliate organizations are often referred to by acronyms. I spell out the affiliates and sometimes double-post but not always. It depends on the space limitations and on how close together in the index the acronym and the spelled-out version fall.

CONCEPTS, LAWS, AND LEGAL CASES

Aside from names, the other indexable materials in these sorts of books are laws, legal cases, and concepts. There are often section headers in the text, but, as in other scholarly books, those may or may not be helpful. I tend to look at the lead sentence of a paragraph for help. Some terms get a little long. I get textbooks about government that are fairly well structured as well as policy reviews on specific subjects that are more narrative and not as tightly structured. I've indexed books on capital punishment, tobacco regulation, welfare policy, and European Union expansion. Some of these public policy books are also about economics, such as microfinance programs or how the former Soviet Union countries are coping with capitalism. It can be pretty fascinating.

In multi-authored works, the first chapter usually provides an introduction that reviews the contents of the book. Each chapter is reviewed, and the author of each chapter is named. The publisher has indicated I should index this chapter so I put those names in the index along with the concepts named. Many people index this chapter much later, but I tend to leap right into trouble and tackle it first. Yes, I often have to revise my terminology since the writer of the overview often characterizes the chapter author's concepts in slightly different ways.

NOTES AND APPENDIXES

The question of whether to index appendixes and notes is important to determine. Some publishers feel notes are superfluous material. They assume that if the material in the notes were central to the text, it would be in the main part of the book. Once when I was indexing a long book on the Kennedy assassination with too little time to complete it, I decided not to index the notes using this point of view as my guide. That was the wrong choice that time! So it's good to ask.

I have one publisher-client who has a particularly convoluted method for locators for notes. These are usually endnotes, and the publisher primarily wants the scholars' names picked up. If a scholar is mentioned just once on a page, then the locator (for this publisher) will be like this: 95 *n*27. But if a scholar is mentioned more than once, the locator could look like this: 108 *nn*27, 28, 29, 32, 48.

Mixing the two together makes my eyes glaze over. It's like dying a slow death by numbers, but that's what they want so I provide it for them. Indexing software wants to consider the note numbers as page numbers so I always have to code these to have the software ignore everything from the first comma to the last note number. Often I have the added wrinkle of having to index from first page proofs and not second ones, so I have to cope with dummy page numbers. That section in my software manual is heavily marked up with cautions. I have nightmares when changing dummy page numbers to real page numbers that have ended up scrambling the note numbers. Be careful and test your changes before you do them for a lot of page numbers.

The italicized "*n*" in the page locator for these notes drives me crazy, so as I'm indexing I put them in as roman text and not italicized text. Then when I finish the data entry, I find the letter "n" in the page field and replace it with an "*n*." That's an efficiency that saves me from insanity. First I make a group of all records with an "n" in the page field. Then I sort those in page order to see how many cross-references I picked up that also contain the letter "n." They'll be at the end in a page-order sort. This may be an unnecessary step but I'm always curious to see how many are included. I make a subgroup from this that includes all records that do *not* have the whole word "see." Again I put it in page order to make sure there are no cross-references left. It's at this point I replace the pattern "n" in a page field with an "*n*" in a page field.

ALPHABETIZATION AND DETAILS

I don't always get index style guides for these books. Sometimes I get a previous index that someone liked to use as a model. They are often, but not always, sorted letter-by-letter. Some editors want the main headings to have an initial cap; most want run-in indexes. Most editors don't want the alphabetical groups to have the letter announcing the start of the section. Run-in style dictates using only two levels. Subentries are always sorted in alphabetical order, so wording is critical. When legal cases are included they are indexed in a shortened form more often that not, such as *Marbury v. Madison* (1803) and are not double-posted for the second party's name (e.g., Madison). Yes, that's a failing, but that's "the way they've always done it." Sometimes the *In re* and *Ex parte* cases are inverted, but those are the only ones given special consideration. Space for the index doesn't seem to be an issue for the most part.

INDEX DELIVERY

Just about everyone is accepting electronic files, and most are happy with receiving them as e-mail attachments. Some editors welcome Rich Text Files (rtf), but some want Quark-ready files. Others want some typesetting codes. I've learned to make typesetting code templates for a few different publishers. They don't always know what they want, but I try to find out what the designer wants. When they don't specify, they get a Rich Text File.

I tend to save up my queries and send a few at a time. Depending on the time I'm given for indexing, I sometimes send my queries all at once at the end. We're indexers, not fact-checkers. Sometimes translators don't spell things the same way twice—even on the same page. If I find I have lots and lots of queries that affect the index, I send a batch at a time and resolve not to work for those people again.

CONCLUSION

The subject matter is often pretty interesting although some books will really bore the general reader. Other subjects may pay better, but I like the subject matter of these books. I got work by sending a functional résumé. I didn't follow up with a phone call. And the work came. Oh, and Harry Truman doesn't have a middle name, just an initial "S." Some publishers prefer to omit the period after that S, so watch out.

REFERENCES

Chicago Manual of Style, 15th ed. 2003. Chicago: University of Chicago Press.
Mulvany, Nancy C. 1994. *Indexing Books*. Chicago: University of Chicago Press.

Chapter 4

Challenges and Resources in Indexing Philosophy

© 2005 Martin L. White

Philosophy differs from all other disciplines in having no external referent. As the Greeks had it, philosophy is thought turning back upon itself. This reflexivity can make it difficult for the uninitiated to understand what philosophers are talking about, and that lack of understanding can make it difficult, or worse, for the non-philosopher to index a philosophical text. All disciplines present problems to the indexer, but the fact that all philosophical discourse is second-level metadiscourse creates, I think, problems unique to it.

As scholarly indexers, we might wish to work only in our areas of expertise, but most of us would have a hard time making a living if we attempted to do so. Further, one of the fringe benefits of scholarly indexing is variety and the opportunity to learn something new. In what follows, I shall attempt to point out some of the problems encountered in indexing philosophy and to review some resources for overcoming them. I restrict the discussion to Western philosophy, though much of what is said will also apply to non-Western philosophy; in the resources section, I shall indicate which works also cover Islamic, Jewish, or Asian philosophy.

TERMINOLOGY
Philosophical Jargon

All disciplines have their jargon, but, as noted above, philosophy is unique in being nothing but jargon. Some philosophical jargon is readily identifiable as such. One would be unlikely to mistake "transcendental unity of apperception," "referential opacity," or "doxastic implication" for garden-variety English. But much philosophical jargon consists not of specially coined words, but of ordinary words used in special, sometimes unusual or even perverse, ways. The following all have technical meaning (or meanings) in philosophy, and, although they might be considered "background" in other disciplines, they are "foreground" and potentially indexable in philosophy: appearance, being (often "Being"), beauty, cause, duty, good (often "the good"), idea, intention, matter, mind, motive, necessity, objectivity, opinion, particular, reality, responsibility, truth, understanding, universal, and will.

Foreign Languages

English is often not the only language encountered in English-language philosophy texts. Many important philosophical concepts have entered the English philosophical vocabulary from other languages, and they are sometimes left untranslated. Most often encountered are terms from Greek, Latin, and German, as well as a smattering of French.

Philosophy as we know it originated in Greece, and many of the names of the subdisciplines (aesthetics, epistemology, ethics, logic, metaphysics, and political philosophy) come from Greek, as well as the word "philosophy" itself ("love of wisdom"). You can still find the occasional Greek word (*logos, nous, ontos, ousia, phusis*) in philosophical texts, usually transliterated, but once in a while in the Greek alphabet.

Latin was the language of scholarship of medieval Europe, and the medieval philosophers left their mark on the philosophical lexicon. However, their philosophical views have fallen out of fashion (except perhaps in Roman Catholic philosophy), and nowadays you are less likely to encounter Latin terms than Greek, though a few, such as *qualia* and *sensibilia,* have retained some currency.

German philosophy has been important since G. W. Leibniz in the 17th century, and the German penchant for neologisms has made itself manifest in the discipline. German philosophical vocabulary is often left untranslated, so that you find the Hegelian *Aufheben* rather than "overcome and preserve" (as J. N. Findlay translates it) or the Heideggerian *Dasein* rather than "being-there" (as it's usually rendered in English).

Logic

Another "language" you encounter in philosophical texts is the language of logic. Logic has been an important part of philosophy since the pre-Socratics. It was central to medieval Scholasticism, and it enjoyed a prominent role in German and Austrian positivism and in Anglo-American analytical philosophy of the post–World War II era. In texts by authors having a logical bent you might encounter:

'$(x)[Hx \equiv RAx]$' is L-true (from Rudolf Carnap, *Meaning and Necessity*)
$(p \ \& \ {\sim}B_a p) \ \& \ {\sim}B_a p(p \ \& \ {\sim}B_a p)$ (from Jaakko Hintikka, *Knowledge and Belief*)
$(x)(y) \ \{(x = y) \supset [\text{necessarily } (x = y)]\}$(from W. V. Quine, *From a Logical Point of View*)

Some familiarity with logical terminology is certainly useful, if not required, to understand a significant portion of the body of philosophical literature (the glossary of philosophical terms in the *Encyclopedia of Philosophy* [see page 41] is helpful), and a knowledge of at least the notation of the propositional and predicate calculi (unfortunately, there are many systems of notation) is required to work comfortably in texts such as those from which the above examples are taken.

Terms from Other Disciplines

Philosophy, as we have said, is "thought turning back upon itself." As thought has historically been organized into various disciplines, so philosophy is often subdivided into branches such as philosophy of art, philosophy of history, philosophy of mathematics, philosophy of religion, philosophy of science, political philosophy, and so on. You can expect, therefore, to encounter terminology from those disciplines in the corresponding branches of philosophy. The language of the discipline at issue will penetrate the philosophical discussion in addition to the strictly philosophical vocabulary. Much of this terminology will be familiar to most scholarly indexers, but, as you would expect, that from the philosophy of science, which is a particularly active field at present, can be daunting to the indexer with a liberal arts background.

Postmodernism/Poststructuralism

For most of the 20th century, philosophy was pretty well isolated from the other disciplines. The particular sciences had established their autonomy by the end of the 19th century, and philosophy, especially in the English-speaking countries, had entered onto the path of logical and linguistic analysis, which often bore little obvious relation to the external world. That isolation was brought to an end with the advent of postmodernism and poststructuralism in the 1970s. Most postmodernist thought is infused with the phenomenological method devised by the German philosopher Edmund Husserl at the beginning of the 20th century and developed by Martin Heidegger in Germany and Jean-Paul Sartre in France, among others. The Frankfurt school of social critics has been a major agent in the spread of the phenomenological approach, as have the French philosophers Jacques Derrida and Michel Foucault. The approach has also been adopted in cultural studies and by many feminist theorists.

The phenomenological method is thought to be applicable to all of human experience, and in its postmodern incarnation it has cropped up in almost all of the humanities and social sciences. If you have indexed in these fields in recent years, you can hardly have avoided it. Phenomenology has been a major source of philosophical jargon (bracketing [*epoch<mac>e*], eidetic reduction, and naturalistic attitude in Husserl; being-there [*Dasein*], being-with [*Mitsein*], and for-world [*Umwelt*] in Heidegger; and being-for-itself [*être-pour-soi*], being-in-itself [*être-en-soi*], and nihilate [*néantir*] in Sartre), though little of it has filtered down into the recent scholarly applications of the method. What has filtered down is a delight in neologism and turgid and convoluted prose that is difficult, if not impossible, to read and that seems to defy indexing. (An indexer told me the following joke: What do you get when you cross a postmodernist and a Mafioso? An offer you can't understand.)

The following passage from Sartre's *Being and Nothingness* (translated by Hazel Barnes, Philosophical Library) is an example of phenomenological analysis and prose:

> Husserl tells us that the reflected-on "gives itself as having been there before reflection." But we must not be deceived here; the *Selbständigkeit* of the not-reflected-on qua not-reflected-on in relation to all possible reflection does not pass into the phenomenon of reflection, for the phenomenon loses its character as not reflected-on.

I recall seeing a posting on the indexers' listserv that stated that the indexer would no longer accept postmodernist books. I never went that far, though I did joke about declaring a moratorium on indexing the name Foucault. It appears that the postmodernist fad is waning. Not long ago it seemed that every other book took the postmodernist approach, but I've hardly indexed Foucault in months. For whatever postmodernist work is still out there, be advised: it's going to be hard to understand and it's going to take longer than usual to index. Regardless of the fate of poststructuralism, phenomenology, having taken root in American philosophy departments, will be presenting indexing challenges for some time to come.

ARGUMENTS

So far, I've discussed words. Words are perhaps the indexer's first concern, and selecting them for index headings is perhaps the indexer's first and foremost task. But there's more to philosophy than terminology. Philosophy is also concerned with arguments. Some would argue that it is nothing but arguments. Philosophy is not unique in containing arguments. Most scholarly books consist of a thesis and an argument or arguments to establish that thesis. But because philosophy has no direct reference to the external world, philosophers can't appeal to empirical evidence to support their positions. They have recourse only to arguments. It's the indexer's job to see that the author's arguments are reflected in the index.

There are two aspects of philosophical argument that I want to address. First is the relatively simple issue of named arguments. There are some arguments in the history of philosophy that are of such significance that they have had names bestowed on them. Among them are the various paradoxes of Zeno, the medieval Buridan's Ass argument, the cosmological, ontological, and teleological arguments for the existence of God, and the Cartesian *cogito ergo sum* argument. I say that named arguments are a simple issue, because a good author (from the indexer's point of view, at least) will call them by their names. If you're in doubt as to whether you have one of them, some of the sources below may be of use.

Second, philosophical arguments tend to be abstract and complex. As we've seen above, they sometimes employ ordinary words in extraordinary ways. It would be a lot to expect of an indexer that he or she master the argument of the book before creating the index. Fortunately, I don't think that mastery of the argument is required. The indexer certainly doesn't have to determine whether the argument is sound. After all, many of them probably aren't. Most arguments of any interest have been around, in one form or another, for millennia, and philosophers aren't in any greater agreement on them today than they were in ancient Greece. What the indexer does need to grasp, however, is the structure of the argument, how the terms fit into premises and conclusion, so that those terms can be fit into corresponding heading–subheading complexes in the index.

PRINT RESOURCES

Even those with philosophical training will require reference works in order to verify a fact or to help them follow an argument. In this section are some resources that should help you to find your way around the world of philosophy. In the next section, I've listed some Internet resources.

Introductions and Histories

There are numerous introductions to and histories of philosophy. Although it's worth keeping one or two on hand, generally they're so short, relative to the ground to be covered, that they're not much use for reference. The nine-volume history by Frederick Copleston, S. J. (Doubleday, $17.95 each), is probably the most substantial and most useful general history of philosophy of the late 20th century.

Encyclopedias

A good general encyclopedia, such as *Encyclopaedia Britannica,* can be useful but can't compare with a specialist encyclopedia. To my knowledge, there are two multi-volume encyclopedias currently available that are devoted entirely to philosophy.

The *Encyclopedia of Philosophy,* edited by Paul Edwards (8 vols., index in vol. 8, Macmillan, 1967; $650) is alphabetically organized. The set now available is in four volumes, with each volume containing two of the original volumes. The *Encyclopedia of Philosophy* was published at the height of the ascendancy of analytic philosophy, but it covers all areas of Western philosophy. There are also articles on Buddhism, Chinese philosophy, Indian philosophy, and Islamic philosophy. A supplementary volume ($130), edited by Donald M. Borchert, was published in 1996 in order to try to keep the set up-to-date. The four-volume set was offered as a premium by some book clubs many years ago, so it may be possible to find a used set. Adding the 1996 supplement could yield a useful reference work at a reasonable price. Both the four-volume set and the supplement are available from Gale.

The *Routledge Encyclopedia of Philosophy*, edited by Edward Craig is 10 volumes including the index volume (Routledge, 1998; $3,495). There are also CD-ROM and online versions. It is alphabetically organized. The *Routledge Encyclopedia* is a monumental work. Like the *Encyclopedia of Philosophy*, it covers all areas of Western philosophy and also has articles on non-Western topics. The articles are substantial, as is the index, which seems reasonably well organized. I don't own this nor do I live close enough to a library that has a copy, so I can't say how it is to work with day-to-day. From what I have seen of it in a university library, it is well worth the price for those who can afford it. Most indexers, however, may prefer the one-volume work by the same publisher (see following section).

Dictionaries and One-Volume Encyclopedias

There are dozens of single-volume dictionaries and encyclopedias of philosophy. Many are quite useful, others useless or worse. What follows is a list of those of which I have at least some first-hand knowledge. I've attempted to list the latest editions, which I may not have seen. I've listed the price when I could find it.

The *Cambridge Dictionary of Philosophy*, edited by Robert Audi (1,001 pp., Cambridge University Press, 2d ed., 1999; $85), is also available in a paperback edition ($29.95). It is alphabetically organized, though many items are actually discussed at the entry for their broader term. Substantial attention is given to non-Western philosophy. There is an index of selected names.

Collins Dictionary of Philosophy, by G. Vesey and P. Foulkes (300 pp., Collins, 1990), appears to be out of print. It is alphabetically organized. The entries tend to be slightly longer than simple definitions. It lacks an index.

The *Concise Encyclopedia of Western Philosophy and Philosophers*, edited by J. O. Urmson and Jonathan Rée (352 pp., Routledge, 3d ed., 1993; $24.95), is a paperback edition. It's alphabetically organized, but many items are discussed in the articles on their broader terms. The cross-referencing is inadequate. I know this work from the Unwin Hyman 1989 edition. Rée has updated the original 1960 edition by the respected Oxford philosopher John Urmson. The articles are skewed toward individuals and movements rather than topics. There is, for example, material on the mind/body problem in the articles on Descartes and the philosophy of mind, but no heading for it. There is no index.

Concise Routledge Encyclopedia of Philosophy (1,030 pp., Routledge, 2000; $42.95), is the one-volume abridgement of the 10-volume set described above. It is alphabetically organized. The emphasis is on individual philosophers, but there are also many entries on philosophical and religious concepts and subjects. There is considerable coverage of non-Western philosophy. There is a substantial analytical index, though I've found many errors and omissions in it.

A *Dictionary of Philosophy,* edited by Antony Flew (400 pp., Random House Value Publishing, 2d ed., 1999; $10), is also a paperback edition. It is alphabetically organized. I know this work from the St. Martin's Press edition of 1984. Flew is a British analytical philosopher and his dictionary reflects that perspective. Short, definitional entries are mixed in with longer, explanatory ones. There are a few entries on non-Western topics. It lacks an index.

A *Dictionary of Philosophy,* edited by Thomas Mautner (482 pp., Blackwell Publishers, 1996), is apparently out of print. Mautner is also editor of the *Penguin Dictionary of Philosophy.* This volume is alphabetically organized and a mixture of short, definitional entries and longer, explanatory ones. Except for entries for Arab and Jewish philosophers, there are few entries on non-Western subjects. There is no index.

Oxford Companion to Philosophy, edited by Ted Honderich (1,009 pp., Oxford University Press, 1995; $60), is alphabetically organized. The entries tend to be slightly longer than straightforward definitions. There is some attention given to non-Western philosophy. The index uses article titles as locators.

The *Oxford Dictionary of Philosophy,* by Simon Blackburn (418 pp., Oxford University Press, 1996; $50), is also a paperback edition. It is alphabetically organized, and the entries are generally short and definitional. It contains some terms from Chinese and Indian philosophy.

Reference Works on Specialized Areas Within Philosophy

The *Biographical Dictionary of Twentieth-Century Philosophers,* by Brown, Collinson, and Wilkinson (947 pp., Routledge, 1996; $200), includes subjects such as Chinese and Indian as well as Western philosophers. Almost as interesting as the entries are the various indexes by nationality, category (schools, movements, and fields), and influences on the philosophers. There are also standard name and subject indexes.

The *Encyclopedia of Asian Philosophy,* edited by Oliver Leaman (669 pp., Routledge, 2001; $160), is alphabetically organized. The articles cover people, schools, and topics in Chinese, Indian, Islamic, Japanese, Korean, Persian, and Tibetan philosophy. There are name and subject indexes.

The *Encyclopedia of Classical Philosophy,* edited by Donald J. Zeyl (632 pp., Greenwood Press, 1997; $110), is alphabetically organized. The relatively long articles are skewed toward people and schools rather than topics. There is an index, but many entries are unanalyzed.

The *Encyclopedia of Empiricism,* edited by Don Garrett and Edward Barbanell (488 pp., Fitzroy Dearborn Publishers, 1997; $105), is alphabetically organized. The longish articles are generally on people or broad topics. There is a short, analytical index.

The *Encyclopedia of Phenomenology,* edited by Lester Embree and others (764 pp., Kluwer Academic Publishers, 1997; $555), is alphabetically organized. The entries are skewed toward names and broad topics. There is an unanalyzed index.

The *Encyclopedia of Postmodernism,* edited by Victor E. Taylor and Charles E. Winquist (466 pp., Routledge, 2001; $125), is alphabetically organized. The entries are skewed toward individuals and broad topics. There is an analytical index.

INTERNET RESOURCES

There is, as you would expect, a large amount of information about philosophy available on the Internet. Like most information on the Internet, it is often of unknown pedigree, and it changes often and without notice. The list of sites that follows consists of those that I've found useful and interesting. It is not intended to be comprehensive.

Search Engines and Web Guides

The various search engines yield a great many links for philosophy. Yahoo (Arts-Humanities-Philosophy) groups its links under categories such as books, organizations, and philosophers, and by the branches of philosophy and other high-level headings. AltaVista (Home-Directory-Library-Humanities-Philosophy) organizes its links in categories such as history of philosophy, philosophers, and philosophy by topic. Google returns "about 6,870,000" links, but without any apparent organization.

Web Sites

In the following, the addresses in parentheses consist of the part of the address following http://.

The Dictionary of Philosophy of Mind (artsci.wustl.edu/~philos/MindDict) is edited by Chris Eliasmith (Washington University, St. Louis). This is a short and not very comprehensive (e.g., no entry on identity theory) glossary of terms from the philosophy of mind. The entries consist of a short definition, explanatory material of varying length, and references. There is an alphabetical index and a search utility.

EpistemeLinks.com (www.epistemelinks.com) is maintained by Thomas Ryan Stone, a philosophy graduate who now works in computers. The site contains philosophy-related links grouped under two main categories, Philosophers and Topics (which is subdivided into Historical Time Periods, Philosophical Subject Areas, Schools and Traditions, and Practicing Philosophy), and subsidiary categories such as E-texts, Organizations, Publishers, and Other Link Sites. There is a useful navigational system.

Garth Kemerling's Philosophy Pages (www.philosophypages.com) is maintained by Garth Kemerling (Newberry College). The site contains a summary of the history of Western philosophy, a dictionary of philosophical terms and names (which consists of short definitions and references), a time line of Western philosophers (which includes Arab philosophers), biographical entries for a good number of philosophers, a brief summary of logic, a study guide for philosophy, and links to other philosophy sites on the Internet.

The Internet Encyclopedia of Philosophy (www.utm.edu/research/iep) is edited by James Fieser (University of Tennessee at Martin) and Bradley Dowden (California State University, Sacramento). The encyclopedia consists of a time line of Western philosophy, an alphabetically organized series of articles on topics in Western philosophy, and a list of key words that reference the articles (this latter serving as an index). The list of subjects covered is a bit spotty at present, but with time it may become more comprehensive. There is a glossary of terms of what the editors call Eastern Philosophy. The navigational system could be improved.

Kant on the Web (www.hkbu.edu.hk/~ppp/Kant.html) is edited by Steve Palmquist (Hong Kong Baptist University). This site includes digital versions of some of Kant's works, links to sites containing digital versions of other works, an index for Norman Kemp Smith's translation of the *Critique of Pure Reason* (alas without analysis), links to online articles about Kant, a glossary of Kant's technical terms, and even some images of the philosopher.

Noesis Philosophical Research online (noesis.evansville.edu) is maintained by the University of Evansville. It provides searching of online philosophy texts, including essays, lectures, reviews, journals, and several Internet encyclopedias (the Dictionary of Philosophical Terms and Names, Dictionary of the Philosophy of Mind, Internet Encyclopedia of Philosophy, and Stanford Encyclopedia of Philosophy). There is a topic index for restricting your search.

Stanford Encyclopedia of Philosophy (plato.stanford.edu) is edited by Edward N. Zalta (Center for the Study of Language and Information, Stanford University). The editorial board consists of philosophers from many American universities. The encyclopedia consists of an alphabetically organized series of substantial articles on topics in world philosophy (though the emphasis is Western). When completed, it will be a very useful resource, but at present only a small percentage of the articles projected are actually written. There is also a search utility.

xrefer (www.xrefer.com) is a site that searches encyclopedias, dictionaries, thesauri, and other reference works. For philosophy, it searches the *Oxford Companion to Philosophy*, returning links to all of the articles from that work that contain the search terms.

News Groups and Mailing Lists

There are many Internet news groups dedicated to philosophy and philosophers (e.g., alt.philosophy, alt.philosophy.kant) and a large number of listserv mailing lists (for a current list, check www.lsoft.com). Yahoogroups.com also hosts several groups on philosophical topics.

CONCLUSION

The necessity of specialist knowledge is an eternal question in indexing. Indexers, for the most part, are generalists, and subject-matter specialists, for the most part, aren't indexers. The amount of subject knowledge required to create an acceptable index probably varies by field. It's my impression that, in the humanities, philosophy, because it is self-contained and has a propensity for technical jargon, probably requires more background knowledge than most other fields. In the first section, I've attempted to give an overview of the language of philosophy and of philosophical argument. Although even the quick-study might find that it will take awhile to get up to speed in understanding philosophical jargon and argument (and those with training in philosophy will always be encountering something new), I think that with persistence and reference tools of the sort listed in the second section, most indexers can acquire the philosophical background to create adequate, or better, indexes for philosophical texts.

Chapter 5

Indexing Economics

© 2005 Mary Mortensen

The scope of this chapter encompasses economics in a broad sense, including the topics of finance, political economy, and economic history. Although economics has a reputation of being a boring or obscure subject, I find that most of the topics of scholarly economics books can be related to real-life issues and therefore are not boring at all. School financing and environmental protection are issues that we may deal with in our own communities. Government budgets, taxes, globalization, and the financial markets appear in the news every day. Economic history can be as exciting as other types of history.

BACKGROUND KNOWLEDGE AND REFERENCES

I started indexing economics books because I had studied the subject in college and graduate school (my master's is in international relations, not pure economics, however) and had worked in large international banks for 13 years. This background makes me comfortable with the terminology and approach of scholarly economics books. While educational and work experience are extremely helpful for indexers of economics books, as in most fields, there are ways for indexers to get sufficiently comfortable with economics to start indexing in it.

The readers of scholarly economics books will generally be professors, researchers, or graduate students and will share a great deal of background knowledge on economics concepts and the relationships among them. It is therefore important that the indexer be aware of the meanings of basic economics terms, their relationships and synonyms. Sources for definitions include books, Web sites, and the news media.

Basic economics textbooks are available at libraries and college bookstores. Popular economics and finance books written for general audiences are also useful. If an indexer can start in the economics field by indexing textbooks or trade books on basic economics topics, these should provide a sense of the terminology used in the field and can be a useful background for indexing scholarly economics books.

Reference sources are also valuable. There are several paperback economics dictionaries available in bookstores. Web sites with economics glossaries or dictionaries can also be useful, although they may not have been as carefully verified as published books.

Examples of economics glossaries on the Web include:

www.economicswebinstitute.org/concepts.htm
www.econterms.com

If these Web addresses no longer work when you try them, other economics glossaries can be found by looking at general reference Web sites or lists of glossaries, such as www.glossarist.com.

It is also very helpful to read about economics topics in the news, especially in newspapers and magazines, which can give more space to explanations of concepts than can television and radio. The *Wall Street Journal*, the business sections of other major newspapers, and business magazines, such as the *Economist* and *Business Week,* publish articles on general economics concepts. I've found that the *Economist* has especially clear explanations. Some publications have most of their content available free online, and newspapers such as the *New York Times* (www.nytimes.com) keep special financial stories and sections on their Web sites for a few months.

TERMINOLOGY

An indexer with economics knowledge will be able to identify the terms in the text that readers will likely use in searching the index. As in other types of books, context can be important. For example, the term "development" in the context of local real estate has a different meaning than in the context of national economies. A book about the U.S. economy will have few subheadings under "United States" while a book about international economics will have many country names, including the United States, with similar subheadings (e.g., trade agreements, imports, exports).

Subject knowledge is also helpful in understanding when a topic falls into a broader subject. For example, in books dealing with national policies, discussions of taxes should also be indexed under "fiscal policy" (or a cross-reference should be created), while in books on microeconomics, the broader term will not be applicable.

If the author refers to corporations with the short forms of their names (such as "Ford" instead of "Ford Motor Company"), the full names should be found in reference books or on the Web. I have found Hoover's Online (hoovers.com) useful for this purpose.

SYNONYMS AND CLOSELY RELATED TERMS

Economics uses many terms that are synonyms or nearly synonymous. In many cases, the meanings of terms depend on the context. It is important to realize that terms that are synonyms in one book (such as "income," "revenues," and "sales") may refer to distinct but related concepts in another.

The indexer should follow the author's choice of terms but should include *See* cross-references for commonly used synonyms. For example:

> Labor unions. *See* Unions
> Organized labor. *See* Unions
> Trade unions. *See* Unions

It is often useful (but again depends on the book) to link closely related terms with *See also* cross-references. A common example is the group of terms related to employment, such as:

> careers
> employees
> employers
> employment
> jobs
> labor
> labor markets
> occupations
> unemployment
> workers

If, for example, "jobs" and "careers" have distinct meanings in the text, both should be main headings, but it helps the reader to include *See also* cross-references from one to the other.

INDEX STRUCTURE

Scholarly economics books that are focused on very specific topics frequently include discussions of complex relationships among various factors, resulting in a complex index structure. The indexer's task of creating a clear structure is often constrained by being limited to only one level of subentry.

Each of the factors discussed should be a main heading. The relationships usually become subheadings of the factors, but in some cases there are too many page numbers and the relationships need to be made separate main entries. In cases like this, be sure to include cross-references from the factors to the relationship entries. (If the main headings for the factor and the relationship are immediately adjacent in the index, the cross-reference may be eliminated.)

The following example comes from the index to a book on the role of education funding in public school performance. The author discussed several measures of school performance and their relationships to school funding and to each other. The main headings for these factors are:

Earnings
Educational attainment
Education expenditures
Per pupil expenditures
Pupil/teacher ratio
School resources
Standardized tests
Student performance
Teacher education
Teacher salaries

The complicated discussion resulted in a multifaceted index structure. A few of the relationships are shown below in subheadings, cross-references, and new main headings. (Each of these main headings also has other subheadings.)

Earnings
    relationship to standardized test scores
    See also School resources/earnings relationship; Educational attainment/earnings relationship
Educational attainment
    relationship to student performance
    See also School resources/educational attainment relationship
Educational attainment/earnings relationship
    influence of pupil-teacher ratio
Pupil/teacher ratio
    relationship to educational attainment
    relationship to future earnings
School resources
    See also Per pupil expenditures; Pupil-teacher ratio
School resources/earnings relationship
School resources/educational attainment relationship
School resources/student performance relationship
Standardized tests
    relationship of scores to earnings
Student performance
    relationship to attainment
    See also School resources/student performance relationship; Standardized tests
Teachers
    See also Pupil-teacher ratio

The wording of these complex subheadings is important. They should be as concise as possible and the indexer should pick strong keywords to place at the beginning of main headings and subheadings, if possible without making the wording very awkward.

EQUATIONS

The good news is that, in my opinion, the indexer does not need to understand the math in equations in economics books. The concept under analysis in the equation should be in the index, but usually I do not include a subheading of "equation" or a similar term. However, if a model or theorem has a name, it should be indexed. The name is sometimes the last name of the economist or economists who devised the model, or it may refer to the concept explained in the model. Whether this name is well known or invented by the author, readers may look for it in the index, and it should therefore be included.

The parameters of the equation are usually the factors whose relationship is modeled by the equation. They should be indexed where they are defined, but the letters or symbols used in the equation are not needed in the index. Often the variables are then discussed in the explanation of the results of the analysis and should also be indexed on those pages. It is not necessary to index the sample populations or standard model parameters, even if they are named for an economist such as Pareto.

FIGURES AND TABLES

Economics books often include tables, graphs, or other figures. The publisher may have a policy about whether these should be indexed, and if so, how the locators should be formatted (see, for example, *The Chicago Manual of Style*, 15th ed. 2003, sec.18.117; Mulvany 1994, pp. 94–95). If the indexer is not aware of the publisher's policy, he or she should query the editor.

If the figures and tables are to be indexed, usually only the main topic is indexed, not the details within them. There are exceptions, however, such as a table that lists important information about trade agreements that does not appear elsewhere in the text. In addition to indexing the table under "trade agreements," it would also be posted under the name of each agreement (Mulvany 1994, p. 48). Indexing tables at this level of detail should not be done without consulting the editor, however.

SUMMARY

Scholarly economics books present challenges similar to other scholarly books in the need for knowledge of the subject area and in the complexity of the texts. To me, the main differences arise from the need to address the vast number of synonyms used by economists and the mathematics used in some economics books.

REFERENCES

Chicago Manual of Style, 15th ed. 2003. Chicago: University of Chicago Press.
Mulvany, Nancy C. 1994. *Indexing Books*. Chicago: University of Chicago Press.

Chapter 6

Foreign Language Issues in Scholarly Indexing

© 2005 Nedalina (Dina) Dineva

Foreign language issues are bound to come up in any scholarly text. History books might refer to organizations or political systems by the names used in their country of origin. Anthropology books commonly use terms derived from different cultures to capture unique social structures. Literary criticism texts often cite titles of works that either do not have an English translation or the translation does not capture the full meaning of the original.

Although the indexers of scholarly books are not expected to be polyglots, it is desirable that they have some basic knowledge of the most widely used languages. At the very least, indexers need to know how to treat diacritical marks, personal names, titles of works, and terms borrowed from other languages.

DIACRITICS

The most common encounter with foreign language vestiges, even in a simple author index, involves diacritical marks. Diacritical marks are embellishments (dots, bars, squiggly lines, etc.) of roman letters that indicate special pronunciation or stress in the original language. Although the diacritics do not change the alphabetization of words (they are treated just like their English equivalents for sorting purposes), they should not be ignored in the index. In fact, special care should be taken to represent the diacritics accurately since their omission or slight variation could result in a change of meaning.

If your indexing software does not allow you to represent a diacritic exactly as it appears, you should create a code for it, while making sure that the correct alphabetical order is preserved. For example, if you cannot represent the letter "ä" using your indexing software, you might code the word "Realität" as "Realit{a}<&adoubledot;>t." (Alternatively, if you want to show your erudition, you could use the technical term and code ä as <&adieresis;>.) The curly braces indicate that "a" should be evaluated for sorting, but it should be hidden in the formatted view. The angle brackets have the opposite function: the letters enclosed in them are ignored for sorting, but they are shown in the formatted view. Thus your entry will look like this: Realit&adoubledot;t. Of course, the final printed index cannot contain such gobbledygook. Either the typesetter or you, the indexer, will have to convert the code to the actual symbol. If you choose the first option, you should provide the typesetter with a list of the codes you have used and the symbols that correspond to them. Yet, the second option is no more time-consuming and easily attainable in most cases.

If you have a relatively recent word-processing program, you should have access to most of the diacritics that you encounter. Save your index as a word-processing file, open it in your word-processing program, and search for "& and ;" (these are used to distinguish your codes from other strings of characters). Then replace the codes with the actual letters containing the diacritics. In Microsoft Word you can access special characters under Insert and then Symbol. However, this will only allow you to replace one code at a time. In indexes with many coded characters, you might want to use the Character Map. It can be found by clicking on the Start button on your desktop, then on Accessories, System Tools, Character Map. The Character Map will allow you to select and copy symbols, which you can then paste into the "Replace with" window of Word's Find and Replace function. In this way you can substitute all the codes for a particular diacritic with just one stroke (assuming that the coding was done consistently). Granted, this is a bit more work than pure indexing, but it is well worth taking this extra step to make sure that the client receives a usable, professional-looking product.

PERSONAL NAMES

The ability to distinguish initial articles and prepositions in another language becomes paramount in the filing of personal names. In French names containing prefixes, for example, the decision of which part of the name to use for sorting depends on separating the article from the preposition within the prefix. Articles and contractions of articles and prepositions are used for alphabetizing, while prepositions are ignored and placed at the end. Thus, "Julien Offroy de La Mettrie" is filed as "La Mettrie, Julien Offroy de"; "George du Maurier" (where "du" is a contraction of the preposition "de" and the article "le") is filed as "du Maurier, George"; while "Alexis de Tocqueville" is indexed as "Tocqueville, Alexis de." Similar rules apply to German, Spanish, and Arabic names. Since there is some disagreement over these rules, the primary guide for the indexer should be how the person in question is best known or referred to in the text. If there is variation in the usage of a person's name, appropriate cross-references should be provided. For example, in a book on the history of mathematics, the author consistently refers to Jean Le Rond d'Alembert as "d'Alembert." Obviously, this version of the name should make it into the index—either as a cross-reference to the standard form "Alembert, Jean Le Rond d'" or as the main entry to which "Alembert" has been cross-referenced. (For an extensive discussion, refer to *The Chicago Manual of Style*, 15th ed., pp. 779–782 [sections 18.74–18.85]; Mulvany 1994, pp. 152–182; Wellisch 1996, pp. 354–377.)

TITLES OF WORKS

The ability to distinguish initial articles also comes into play when indexing titles of works in foreign languages. Here, however, the rule is the opposite of that for treating personal (and geographical) names: the initial article is ignored for sorting. The exact treatment depends on the indexer's (and the publisher's) preference: the article can either be transposed (placed at the end of the title) or it can remain in its natural position, with the entry filed under the word immediately following the article. For example, *Der Tod in Venedig* (Mann) could either be left as it appears, but sorted in the Ts or it can be indexed as *Tod in Venedig, Der*. My own experience in following publishers' guidelines and Index-L, an indexing listserv, discussions leads me to conclude that the latest trend favors the former approach because of its more natural appearance. Whichever approach you choose to use, it is important to be consistent in the treatment of English as well as foreign titles; that is, you should either transpose all initial articles or ignore them all for sorting. (An excellent reference table listing the initial articles in major languages appears in Wellisch 1996, p. 240.)

TERMS AND EXPRESSIONS

Another common problem encountered in scholarly texts is the usage of foreign terms as primary carriers of meaning. The authors might decide that the existing English counterpart does not capture the full range of meanings in the original term (e.g., "logos" and "reason/word") or they might consider it impossible to provide an accurate and succinct translation. In such cases, the foreign terms are commonly transcribed in English ("λογοζ" becomes "*logos*") and are italicized in order to distinguish them from the rest of the index entries. The English translation can be provided in parentheses (that is, if a clear translation has been suggested in the text; the indexer is not required to supply the translation if such is missing), and it can also be cross-referenced to the original term.

In some cases, the foreign terms might not be transcribed in the text and can present an especially challenging problem for the indexer if the language used is other than those based on the roman script. An interesting approach to just such a situation can be found in the index for *Collected Dialogues of Plato*, edited by Edith Hamilton and Huntington Cairus (1961). This index, prepared by Edward J. Foye, not only represents a massive analytical undertaking, but it also tackles the added challenge of incorporating ancient Greek terms in their original form. Foye has chosen to include the Greek terms seamlessly in the index by sorting them according to their phonetic (pronunciation) scheme. Thus, "νομοζ" (pronounced "nomos") falls immediately after the entry for "nome" and before "nonexistent one." According to this approach, the original Greek alphabetical order is ignored in the main entries, but not within the entry for "etymology," where all ancient Greek terms appear as subentries and are sorted in the order of the Greek alphabet.

While unusual, Foye's approach to the index is quite logical and functionally compatible with the nature of the book. Most modern readers of philosophy have only rudimentary knowledge of ancient Greek and cannot be expected to move easily within that language's alphabetical system. Yet, for students of philosophy some key ancient Greek terms (e.g., "αρετη," "λογοζ," "νοῡζ") acquire special prominence and exist almost on an equal footing with English concepts. For this audience, the most natural way of looking for ancient Greek terms in the index would be according to their pronunciation. On the other hand, grouping all of the foreign terms under one entry (in this case "etymology," but in another book it could well be "Chinese terms" and "Korean terms") provides another access point to the information for the more linguistically savvy reader. In such an entry, the Greek alphabetical order takes precedence as the more natural way of sorting the exclusively foreign terms.

FOREIGN LANGUAGE TEXTBOOKS

Sometimes the foreign language takes over the very nature of the book and becomes a central concern for the index. Such is the case with foreign language textbooks.

Unique problems are presented by the indexing of foreign language textbooks, especially for languages that use nonroman scripts (e.g., Arabic, Chinese, Greek, Hebrew, Japanese, Russian). Since one of the latest trends in language studies is to provide as much of the information as possible in the foreign language, with explanations in the native language used only as needed, the index also has to become a seamless weave of both languages. It is this coexistence of foreign and English terms that poses some of the greatest challenges for the indexer. The following discussion based on my experience with Russian language textbooks can easily be applied to other non-Western languages.

In my first assignment involving a Russian language textbook, I was asked to prepare a single index that contained both English and Russian terms, reflecting the relationships delineated in the text. The immediate problems I had to resolve were (1) how to represent the letters of the Russian alphabet in the index and (2) what sorting system to use.

The Russian Alphabet

The Russian language uses Cyrillic script, which is quite distinct from the roman script adopted by most Western languages. Although the individual Cyrillic letters could be found in the symbols table of the indexing software I use (CINDEX), I knew that it would be an incredibly slow process to input each of them either by searching in the symbols table or by typing in the appropriate codes. Instead, I decided to use transliteration (i.e., to represent the Russian words in roman script by substituting each of the original letters with one or more roman letters). Then, after I had finished all the manipulations in CINDEX, I could export the file to word-processing software, change the language and keyboard settings to Russian, and replace all my transliterations with the actual Cyrillic script. This process was facilitated by a strict typographical distinction that I carried over from the text: Russian words were represented in boldface, English words or phrases that appeared as examples were in italics, and standard conceptual entries were in roman type. Thus, it was relatively easy for me to distinguish the Russian words from the English ones during the several stages of index manipulation.

Sorting Principle

The second issue that needed to be resolved was that of alphabetical order. Not only does the Russian language use a different script than English, but even similarly sounding letters have a different position in the alphabet. For example, the English "v" corresponds phonetically to the Russian "в," yet the latter appears at the very beginning (position three) in the Russian alphabet rather than close to the end as in English. Clearly, the simple rule for sorting diacritics by using the closest phonetic and graphical equivalent in English could not be used here. A whole new sorting system had to be established, explained, and followed closely.

The first decision I made was to use only English terms in the main entries, followed, where necessary, by the Russian term in parentheses. In this way I could reduce at least the main structure of the index to a single alphabet. I wanted to avoid intermixing the two languages in the first level of entries, even though, as we saw in the example with Plato's dialogues, this can be done quite successfully. Yet, since the users of this textbook are students of a foreign language, I considered preserving and honoring the principles of the Russian language as paramount in the index. On the other hand, I had to employ Russian terms extensively in the subentries in order to reflect the focus on Russian usage in the text. To create some order within the subentries, I postulated that the English alphabet will take primacy in sorting and the Russian alphabet will be considered only after the English one has been exhausted. I explained this principle in the following note at the beginning of the index: "Unless preceded by an English term, Russian words are placed at the end of the entry and are sorted in the order of the Russian alphabet."

In order to follow this principle while working in CINDEX and while using the transliterations of the actual Russian words, I had to force the sorting with hidden codes, so that Russian "v" would actually sort at the beginning of the list. This switching back and forth between the two alphabets posed an interesting mind puzzle, which at times led to frustration as I caught myself slipping into the wrong alphabet.

Example

Below is an excerpt from the actual index:

abbreviations
> in addresses, 253—254
> in names of institutions (**им.**), 137n2
> for number (‹), 118n9

able (**мо**˜ ˍ), 203
> past tense of, 324—325

accent. *see* stress

absence, expressing
> in future tense (**Не** · **y‰ ет** + Genitive case), 267
> in past tense (**Не** · ˍıÎ **o** + Genitive case), 267
> in present tense (**нет** + Genitive case), 131—132

As you can see, the functions of this type of index border those of the grammar book and the dictionary. In addition to the regular conceptual entries (e.g., "absence"), I had to organize the information by its grammatical role (e.g., "abbreviations"). The numerous specific examples in the text had to be included in the index as well (e.g., "able"), thus breaking the rule against listing adjectives or verbs as main entries. In this way, the index resembled a dictionary, yet it went beyond the simple defining role of a dictionary since the focus here was on usage and grammar rather than on explanation of meaning.

The index to a foreign language textbook functions not only as a finding tool but also as instructional material. Since all related information is grouped together, the index can very well be used as a study guide. What such an index requires is an understanding of the students' needs and a strict organization that, to a certain extent, mimics the neural connections that the student has to make in learning the language.

CONCLUSION

Foreign language text encountered in scholarly books does not have to be intimidating or overwhelming even if the language is unfamiliar to us. The basic principles of dealing with foreign characters, names, and titles are easy to follow once we have devoted sufficient time to studying and comprehending them. Yet a general acquaintance with, and affinity for, languages is a great aid in crafting the scholarly index. As in other specialized subject areas, the indexer's holistic knowledge and experience can come to her rescue in the treatment of foreign language issues.

REFERENCES

Chicago Manual of Style, 15th ed. 2003. Chicago: University of Chicago Press.

Hamilton, Edith, and Cairus, Huntington, eds. 1989. *Collected Dialogues of Plato*. 14th ed. Princeton, NJ: Princeton University Press.

Mulvany, Nancy C. 1994. *Indexing Books*. Chicago: University of Chicago Press.

Wellisch, Hans H. 1996. *Indexing from A to Z*. 2d ed. New York: H. W. Wilson.

Chapter 7

Scholarly Indexing in an Unknown Language

© 2005 Jennifer Rushing-Schurr

You must do the thing you think you cannot do. – Eleanor Roosevelt

"My editor is sending me a project that includes a chapter in a foreign language that I don't know. What do I do? Help!"

Calm down. I can help. I have done this. I am not an expert, but I am an expert in not being an expert. I can help you evaluate your skills and decide what to do, and I can guide you through the process of reading and indexing the foreign text yourself. I have been in exactly this situation and survived. I was put on the spot, with no apparent alternative, and as far as the publishers were concerned it was my problem, not theirs. So I undertook a foreign-language index when I had little or no training in the language. My background, education, and profession had given me an assemblage of skills and metacognitive strategies on which I could rely even in an arena where I lacked experience.

Sometimes in this situation you can pass the job off to someone better qualified; sometimes you can arrange to hire another person; but sometimes you are the only one who can get the job done. You are the reader's only hope of getting access to the information contained in that material. What to do? I can help. But first let me tell you how I got into such a predicament, and how I handled it.

IN AT THE DEEP END

What's the easiest way to get yourself into deep water? Jump in after somebody else. Several years ago a colleague of mine was working on a series of multiauthor history volumes: very detailed, very demanding, with very stringent publisher's requirements. He seemed to actually writhe in pain as each new volume arrived, tormented by the impossible burden of mastering each one. And then one showed up with a chapter in Spanish! We panicked, found a Spanish-capable indexer, paid him lots of money, and, being unable to evaluate the result, moved on. Everything was fine for eight or ten volumes and then . . . two chapters in French.

Now, my colleague was an example of someone who shouldn't attempt this method, and he knew it. We had both studied French, but he was devoted to grammar and was picky, cautious, a perfectionist—invaluable in the classroom, but handicapped in the real, fast-moving world. He knew he was utterly incapable of handling translation or indexing in French, so I said I would translate it, or at least provide the gist of it for him. My complementary language gifts run to vocabulary and holistic sense, perhaps a bit weak on grammar and the finer details, but trusting in the power of language and human communication with a carefree confidence that can irritate the perfectionist to no end—but does get the job done. I knew I could at least make a fair representation of the text for him. Attempting the translation whole cloth for later indexing was not very successful, however (see below), so in frustration I said I would just *do* the index for that chapter myself. (I had at that time almost no experience in scholarly indexing, so that made for yet another stratum of water above me.)

I dived in on my rescue mission, floundered, gasped, managed to keep my head above water and my senses about me sufficient to spot names and sieve concepts. (Two years of studying French "for reading knowledge" culminating in a contentious group translation of *Phèdre* does not qualify anyone four years later to translate an article on the charity hospitals of Montreal.) The results were very rough, but there wasn't time or money to bring in expert help, and the publisher was not interested in supplying any of those resources. Do your best, we were told; so we did.

A few volumes later, just when I was starting to gain some confidence with the series' requirements as well as with the French language, along came another chapter in Spanish.

We didn't feel that hiring it out had worked well the first time. But I was doing so well with the French—and who hasn't been exposed to a little Spanish, on the streets, at the grocer's—why not give it a try?

I have never studied Spanish. I was hardly qualified for the French chapters, but this was a different league. I have, however, studied three other languages, and French is a close relative of Spanish. Lifelong reading has given me a huge vocabulary in English, the most high-powered language in the world, which enables me to recognize a great array of cognates in diverse languages. I have a fundamental love of words that draws instruction and insight to it in the way that true passion does, and I have devoted considerable time to pondering the structure, function, and meaning of language itself. I believed that this background qualified me sufficiently to tackle a language for which I wasn't qualified. So I dug up a University of Chicago dictionary at the second-hand store and jumped in again.

This was so much harder! I could tell how much more elemental the results were, and I made some embarrassing mistakes. But the job got done, as well as I could do it—better and quicker than by any other solution available—and that was what the editor wanted, and what the reader needed.

So over the course of perhaps a dozen articles in French and Spanish, with some longish quotes in Latin and Greek thrown in, I won't say I ever got qualified, but I did gain confidence. My work was providing some service to the reader and was increasing in quality. And I hammered out the approach you'll find below: a rough-and-ready method for emergency situations that is sensitive at each juncture to the peculiar needs of this endeavor. It can be done. Let's look at other options for handling such a project, and then consider whether *you* can do it.

SINK OR SWIM

Most of this article will provide support for undertaking this challenge yourself, but that is not your only option. You do have others.

First, you can hire a professional to translate the material and then index the results yourself. This is a reassuring approach—you can be certain that everything is in order and no concept has been missed—but it is expensive, and may depend on whether the editor is helping you with the costs of this burden. Finding a professional and waiting for the turnaround can also add time to your schedule. Connecting with a professional online, however, can save time if not money. All of the Web sites listed below provide links to human translation services. Having the chapter translated online either mechanically (not recommended) or by humans is an option that simply didn't exist when I started working as an indexer. It can still be expensive, but the speed and reliability it offers may offset the expense in some circumstances. Of course, using an online service presupposes that you have the text in an electronic format. If you're working from page proofs, this could present yet another hurdle.

Second, you can subcontract the article to a foreign-language indexer. In my experience such a person is likely to be hard to find, expensive, and slow. But no doubt the professionals with foreign-language specialties included in ASI's *Indexer Locator* could prove me wrong about one or two of those factors.

Or, third, you can *turn down the job*. You may have trouble perceiving this as a realistic option; many indexers panic at the notion of turning down work. But it really is your choice about what work you will undertake. Shunning and poverty will not instantly ensue, and an intelligent and timely refusal is better in the long run than tardy delivery of a substandard product.

Or you can read and index the foreign-language material yourself. Let's look at who can do this and who can't. I encourage you to evaluate your own character and strengths dispassionately, without having your vision either obscured by vanity or annihilated by humility.

In order to tackle such a project, you have to have some kind of foundation on which to build an understanding of the text. You need at least a nodding acquaintance with the language. Maybe even literally: perhaps you've overheard the conversations of neighbors from Bonn or Buenos Aires. Perhaps you've idly scanned bilingual signage or packaging. Perhaps you've watched subtitled movies or heard pop or folk or classical music from other countries. You've probably been exposed to more of any given one of the Romance languages than you realize. (I don't recommend trying this with a non-Romance language. I had two years' study of Greek, which only just enabled me to undertake a single paragraph when I ran into one, and at that I had much greater recourse to the lexicon than I recommend for this method. Had the quote been any longer it would have exceeded my abilities.)

But a sufficiently broad knowledge of English puts you in command of quite a lot of Latin roots and relations, making you well situated for the Romance languages at least. It may be possible to branch into the Germanic languages from here as well, given their vocabulary overlap with English and the influence that Latin also had over their structures.

In addition, most indexers are lifelong readers, constantly immersed in the play of language and delighting in its tricks and turns. From this you probably already have an affinity for language and a sense of the underlying fundamentals of communication.

To succeed with this approach, you certainly do need to have studied some foreign language, though, and preferably more than one, or have studied the nature of language itself. Either way, you'll need to have already spent some time contemplating the similarities and differences of communication systems, etymology, the essence of grammar . . . even if perhaps this contemplation was occurring at a wordless level, in the struggle to master more than one language. The fruits of this meditative process form the necessary underpinning of a successful attempt.

If you don't recognize yourself in this portrayal, give serious consideration to the other options. If you really can't do it, don't. The situation may call for a savior, but if an honest inventory of your background and skills convinces you that your efforts would be worse than nothing, you must acknowledge that. Hire it out one way or the other, or *tell the editor you can't do it*—every freelancer's most bitter pill, I know, but sometimes, for the sake of the work, it must be swallowed.

On the other hand, if this does describe you—if it resonates with your experiences, pursuits, background, and affinities—then you can do it. If the job has to be done, if the editor is calling on you to save the text for the reader, if it's you or nothing, if it's sink or swim—you can do it.

Don't underestimate your gifts, even if you aren't used to acknowledging them as such. You may not realize you have these skills; you may not have been aware that you were picking up bits and pieces of knowledge during a lifetime love of words. Your gift may be in the form of unconscious accretions rather than "credentials" you can point to—it may be a hunch rather than an argument you can make—but it is still real. Your experience and your skills are valid and valuable.

The bottom line is: either you have it or you don't. If you don't, you must acknowledge that and choose another course. But if you have it, all the misgivings in the world won't change that. And if you have it, you can do it.

HOW TO APPROACH THE TEXT

When I first tackled such a project I tried a three-pass method, separating the translation step from the indexing. This approach involved a great deal of redundant effort, however. So I shifted to a two-pass procedure, marking up the text as I read in French or Spanish and then covering the text again to shape my highlighting and marginalia into well-formed entries after I had used every available clue in the remainder of the text to sharpen my sense of the content. This involves engaging in both the indexer's mind and foreign-language-reader's mind at the same time—and the strain is not merely additive but exponential—but better, I find, to plunge into all the levels of challenge at once.

The general approach is to read (and mark) the English portions of the book first, then read (and mark) the foreign-language material. Next, enter the English part, then cast your entries for the foreign chapter after you have that sensitization to the whole. Then when you edit the whole, you should be able to see how the concepts meld together. This involves two-pass indexing for the English text, as well, with the foreign-language reading occurring between the passes over the English.

This method does take some time, of course. Working with one eye on the clock, as the indexer usually must, becomes counterproductive here. You'll have to set aside some time without distractions and make sure to protect the time so that you'll be able to ease into the project.

Don't have time for two-pass indexing? You shouldn't have taken the project in the first place, then. If you're not fluent in the language, one pass will not produce a usable result. Sure, you could find the proper names—maybe . . .

More comfortable with three-pass indexing, tackling the translation separately? If you've got the time and the stamina, go for it. But before you begin to engage with the foreign-language text, use every available external clue to what the text is about. Scaffold your endeavor as much as you possibly can. Sometimes you will have access to an introduction or abstract in English, which will provide great help as you attack the text. Or such an aid may be present in the foreign language, in which case it is worth looking up every word to obtain a sense of the whole. Here, at least, that effort will pay off in time and stress saved later, although in general I am against excessive dependence on the dictionary. Whatever the language of the introduction or abstract, I recommend looking up its keywords in English-to-foreign so you know any possible synonyms, associated terms, and shades of meaning.

I don't recommend making your second pass over the (English) remainder of the book before *reading* the foreign-language chapter. Doing so can be not so much a scaffold as a straightjacket. You don't want to prejudice your mind too much as to the content of the chapter; on unfamiliar ground, it can be more difficult than usual not to impose your own expectations on the material but to let its meaning be revealed.

Be sure to review in advance the language's own particular pitfalls. Know what elements or forms might negate a sentence without looking like a negative. Be alert for idioms, and watch out for *faux amis* since you'll be relying heavily on cognate recognition. Know how to spot proper nouns and terms whether they look like it or not (in German all nouns are upper-cased; in French even nominalized adjectives are lower-cased—you may not have the clues to which you're accustomed.) There may be other naming pitfalls. Review the target culture's naming and sorting conventions. Fortunately finicky things like mood and tense seldom affect the index— but sensitize yourself to the changing forms of identical verbs, especially *to have* and *to be*. (Often the verbs themselves don't even matter, as long as they're not wriggling into negation.) If there is a narrow subject vocabulary, review it before beginning; if the publisher has provided a controlled vocabulary in English, familiarize yourself with the equivalent foreign terms.

You may want to take 15 minutes to read some bilingual materials to get yourself into the groove. Your bookstore or library will probably have some nice heartening picture books in the kids' section with interlinear translations. Soup! Hugs! The vocabulary may not show up in your text, but the exercise will improve your fluency and your morale.

Got enough tips? Then I'll throw you a line, and you'll be ready to jump in and read.

LIFE PRESERVERS

Looking things up brings us to tools—a chance to acquire more lovely reference books and play with online resources.

Get a dictionary. Do not attempt this without a dictionary. You won't be referring to it constantly but you will need it at your side. I find it awkward to work with online versions, but perhaps I haven't fully adapted to the information age. I still find a dog-earable English-to-foreign, foreign-to-English paperback indispensable. Grammar books and verb cheat-sheets (the N-*Hundred and One Verbs* of your choice) also exist if you can't bear not to be obsessive about that kind of thing. If you are working in a specialized vocabulary, you may find it worth the money to pick up a jargon dictionary as well.

There are many, many translation resources on the Web. A handful of the most reputable and useful sites I could find are provided at the end of the article.

TOTAL IMMERSION

Now you're ready to read in a foreign language. Begin by relaxing. Don't think about outcomes or deadlines or grammar; don't worry about catching concepts or spotting names. Just let your mind sink into the text without distance or judgment, just see it, just *be in it*.

In reading in English, reading for pleasure, there is a self-forgetting that occurs, an effortless entry into the world of the book. The reader just plunges in. The indexer begins by using that reader's art to *get* the text, fairly and fully. The first step in indexing is an honest confrontation with the text itself: What does it say? But the indexer must then take that facility and balance it with a rational perspective on the text: How shall I say what it says? This is the adjustment stage, where the content, while fairly represented, can be shaped to the audience, the format, the density, perhaps a controlled vocabulary. The pendulum swings between receptivity and classification, engagement and judgment. This involves the same interplay of skills as between the word lover and the grammarian, the generator and the censor, the rough-hewer and the shaper of ends—but held within one mind, a cat's cradle drawn between right brain and left.

You already know how to read and how to read and index. Reading and indexing in a foreign language just takes those skills and adds another dimension. The reader-indexer working with a foreign language must maintain an even more challenging set of elements in that dynamic equilibrium. But if you can get into a book, you can do this. All you have to do is let yourself sink into the text, trusting it to bear you up. Enter the data stream and let it take you where it will. Then the well-trained data-retrieval part of your mind can kick in.

Yes, I'm talking about not looking up every word. I'm talking about whole-language "reading" of a text you can't read. And just as children are hindered in their comprehension by constantly having their attention redirected toward perfectionism, so you must let go during this stage of the rational, censoring mind. The human brain has an awesome power to assemble meaning from fine clues and similarities and suggestions. Two human beings can communicate without a common language—so too can a lifelong book person communicate with a book without a common language. It may be a clouded and error-prone communication, but in the absence of a better alternative, it will suffice.

So dive in and read, and paragraph by paragraph—or page by page—when you come up for air, come up gripping those conceptual pearls as tightly as you can. What does it say? Underline, highlight, create marginalia, whatever your usual method is. When you pass over the text again, you can see those pearls in the context of the rest of the book and answer the second question, how shall I say what it says? Then you can perceive and adjust the flow of names and concepts, the organic structure of the whole.

HOME AND DRY

Once you've revised your entries from the foreign-language material in light of the whole text and edited for as much consistency and clarity as possible, your index is done! You're wrung out but proud. You have accomplished an impossible task. You will no doubt be accepting a less-than-perfect outcome, but hey—this method is about embracing your imperfect, instinctive, capable side anyway. If you've thrown your heart into it and done your best, it's good enough. The reader can access more information than they could have without your achievement.

And remember: reading and indexing in a foreign language is a triple challenge, so reward yourself accordingly!

ONLINE RESOURCES

All these sites provide links to human translation services. And they all offer lots of off-task fun for language lovers!

http://www.yourdictionary.com/ – quick lookup for the major languages and links to *several* different options for quick-turnaround human translation.

http://babel.uoregon.edu/yamada/guides.html – a linguist's clearinghouse of language resources on the Web. A smashing array of languages if ever you're hit with something obscure—Cree? Manx? Old Church Slavonic?

http://www.foreignword.com/ – online mechanical translation of "small" texts, and quick-button access to multiple dictionaries.

http://www.ilovelanguages.com/ – games and tools and links to *lots* of languages.

Chapter 8

Confessions of an Author-Indexer

© 2005 John Bealle

In sum, rare indeed is the author who can compile a good index.
-Hans Wellisch

When I began freelance indexing, one of my distinct early impressions of the field came from the disdain afforded authors who index their own books. Every book on indexing took care to lecture on the subject; every indexer's Web site seemed to have a special warning for authors who might attempt their own index. The American Society of Indexers (ASI) surely takes the issue seriously, having made available for distribution to authors a brochure entitled "Authors and Indexes: Do It Yourself or Hire a Pro?" This brochure gives a well-balanced view, acknowledging the author's unparalleled grasp of the subject but simultaneously warning that an index is meant for the reader "who may not be as familiar as you with the concepts, thrust, or vocabulary of the topic." Hans Wellisch (1991, p. 17; 1992) surely had the sternest view, providing a catalog of inherent author-indexer deficiencies: lack of indexing training, lack of perspective (too close to the material), propensity to neglect important details, and also, ironically, tendency to overindex. And if these professional admonishments were not enough, there were the offhand comments that compared author indexing to do-it-yourself plumbing or even surgery!

I was both amused and disturbed by this viewpoint, since I had just indexed my own book. My index was a sound and credible effort that even won positive remarks from reviewers, but nonetheless it bore distinct weaknesses that I partly attribute to my status as author. It seems that even the platitudes bore some truth about the shortcomings of author-indexers, but also about the shortcomings of indexers' understanding of authors. Neither of these types of ignorance is a benefit to scholarly indexers, so in this article I intend to redress some of the misunderstandings surrounding authors and author-indexers.

INDEXING *PUBLIC WORSHIP, PRIVATE FAITH*

In some ways, I was not a typical author-indexer. Even though at the time I had not yet anticipated a career in professional freelance indexing, I nonetheless thought of myself as an indexer. When the question arose of indexing my book, it was only minimally an economic one. I'm not sure I would have wanted anyone else to do it.

The book in question was *Public Worship, Private Faith: Sacred Harp and American Folksong* (Athens, GA: University of Georgia Press, 1997). I had written it—as many independent scholarly authors do—partly as professional investment and partly as intellectual necessity. Its subject was American music history. "Sacred Harp" refers to a singing book and to a choral style with ties to vital issues in 18th- and 19th-century American musical culture. The book pertains to the field of folk-lore and ethnomusicology and was acquired by the University of Georgia Press as a title in that subject specialty. So the main readership was at the juncture of these two areas: American music history and folklore/ethnomusicology.

As indexers well know, both author and indexer are key players during the final stages of preparing the book for printing. In my case, this began when I received the copyedited manuscript, and the preparation of the book was put on a tight produc-tion schedule. As an author, this was a time of intense activity (reviewing the copy-editor's work), followed by an idle period waiting while the book is typeset, then followed by the approximately two- or three-week "window," familiar to indexers, of working with the page proofs.

During this idle middle period, as I anticipated doing the index, I began my train-ing as an indexer. Quickly I found my way to Hans Wellisch's *Indexing from A to Z* and Nancy Mulvany's *Indexing Books* and read them very carefully. I was forming in my mind an image of the index and of the process of completing it. By the time the proofs arrived, I had a mature respect for the indexing process and an informed understanding of what a good index looked like. Already, then, I was an atypical author-indexer.

As author and indexer, I received two proof sets—one to proofread, mark up, and return, and the other for indexing. I combined the work, proofreading a page and at the same time recording the index entries for that page. If I knew about indexing software, I didn't own it—I'm certain I used a database-type program that handled the headings and locators reasonably well but required extensive editing and for-matting at the end. I don't recall this as onerous at all, particularly since I planned to do it only once. I also don't recall it having any negative bearing on the index.

Both Wellisch (1991, p. 17) and Mulvany (1994, p. 22) speak of author fatigue as a key factor arguing against the author as indexer. I have talked to authors who attest to this. But one exacerbating factor is that authors may not understand in advance that the index is part of their contractual obligation—the book contract may have been signed years before, when the book was still unwritten, and thus this con-tract provision is long forgotten.

On the other hand, Wellisch and Mulvany underestimate the rejuvenating power of seeing page proofs for the first time, particularly after a period away from the book. Page proofs provide the first glimpse at the graphic design of the book and the first tangible reward for many years of work. Whereas fatigue had indeed affected the final stages of manuscript editing, indexing came at a time of great excitement, with the exhilarating visual pleasure of the book design as the prevailing attitude.

THE AUTHOR'S ADVANTAGE

The initial process of compiling my index passed uneventfully, perhaps owing to the distinct advantage I enjoyed as the book's most knowledgeable reader. Both Wellisch and Mulvany speak favorably of this capacity, and Wellisch (1991, p. 16) notes that some publishers consider authors as "the best-prepared person to index it properly."

Perhaps it would be more precise to say that the author is the best reader. For me, the particular benefits of this came into play at various stages. There was no need for surveying the plan of the book—I knew clearly where the substance of the book was heading at all points. Moreover, it was almost effortless to follow a discourse presented in historical sequence—whose salient theme was the development of musical style—and know at each point its relation to the main substantive issues (e.g., Calvinist theology, Romanticism, the Enlightenment, or Federalism). These topics formed the basis of important main headings in the index.

More importantly, I knew the audience and the field, which provided a perspective for judging the value of the various aspects of passages of text. I may not have been an able representative of naive readers, but I was familiar with the kind of informed readers who comprise the small but loyal readership of many scholarly books. I believe this was crucial knowledge in the ability to distill thematic compass from the book's historical narrative. For example, a naive reader might have been drawn to various aspects of a section about controversies in 18th-century New England choirs, but I thought my readers would likely care about one in particular, "Choirs: as feminized institutions, 23." Or, with the discussion of hymns and psalms, I wanted to engage readers familiar with aspects of the postmodern question of the author:

> Hymns and psalms: text instability of, 14-15, 155, 220-21; translation and imitation of, 14-15; authorial intent vs. attributed sense of, 156; idealized poetic idiom in, 220, 231-36 (*note: subheadings in page order per publisher specs*)

It is not that these themes were entirely absent from the text, but rather that they were embedded in historical narrative that might have distracted someone unfamiliar with the field.

This foreknowledge of the book, the audience, and the field also had a bearing on my facility for reading across the direction of the narrative and identifying themes whose collective significance came more from outside the book than from within. For instance, the theme of "culture writing" appears in various parts of the book even though its significance is not explicitly signaled either by the book's structure or by what would conventionally be thought of as expected topics. That is to say, it is an expected topic in the field. As an "insider" to both the book and the subject area, I was able to bring together discussions of this theme from a variety of contexts:

> Culture writing: as discourse of discovery, 3, 85, 90, 103, 106; and ethnographic realism, 86; irony in, 86, 97, 272-73 (n. 1); objectivity of, 86; outsider status of, 87, 93, 100-101, 111, 193; in newspapers, 93, 181; voyeuristic eye in, 96; verisimilitude in, 96; authorial voicing in, 96, 99; narrative subtexts in, 97, 101; caricature in, 97; dialect in, 98; textural metaphors in, 98, 179-80; confessional style of, 109; serendipity in, 111; as master text, 151; logocentrism and, 181; as discourse of irreconcilable difference, 193 (*note: subheadings in page order per publisher specs*)

This knowledge or point of view did not pertain exclusively to my status as author, of course—it was more a matter of knowledge of the field than of the book. Indeed, I now look back on that index entry as a paradigmatic experience: producing such an entry—where the index transcends the work of the author—is one of the genuine pleasures of the craft of indexing.

EDITING THE INDEX

If knowledgeable reading was the most prominent advantage I enjoyed as an author, lack of experience with indexing technique was the most prominent disadvantage. And of all the shortcomings of this type, my ignorance of editing became the most consequential. Indeed, I'm sure I didn't understand at the time that editing an index constituted a special process at all. As a result, many of the most salient shortcomings of my index could easily have been corrected but, for lack of experience, were not. Since then, learning to edit has made a striking improvement in the quality of my indexes.

The most significant effect of editing has been the ability to correct errors that cannot easily be noticed during the indexing phase. The simplest was the omission of companion locators. The following two entries:

> Baptist Church: in Ohio, 33-34
> Cincinnati: Baptist Church in, 73

could easily have been corrected to read:

Baptist Church: in Ohio, 33-34, 73
Cincinnati: Baptist Church in, 33-34, 73

Or, seeing the entry *"Amazing Grace with Bill Moyers,* 219-21," I did not notice the omission of the companion entry, "Moyers, Bill, 219-21." Experienced indexers know that these sorts of examples are not difficult to find or correct, but my problem came in not knowing to look for them.

There were also instances where I had anticipated the need for cross-references:

Gordon, Larry. *See* Word of Mouth Chorus
Word of Mouth Chorus, 191-94, 196, 263, 280 (n. 5)

During editing, I would have noticed that the "Gordon, Larry" entry with the locators consumed no more space than the cross-reference, and I would have converted the cross-reference to a double-posting: {This is in *The Chicago Manual of Style,* 18.15.}

Gordon, Larry, 191-94, 196, 263, 280 (n. 5)
Word of Mouth Chorus, 191-94, 196, 263, 280 (n. 5)

Similarly, there were cases where the number of locators did not warrant the use of subheads.

Although I included a number of helpful cross-references, I neglected to make a final survey. As a consequence, there were related topics whose connections were left unrecognized. For example, I had entries for "Public school music" and "Singing schools," but no entry that read, "Schools. *See* Public school music; Singing schools."

I also missed the opportunity to combine related subheadings with broader descriptors:

Birmingham: . . . early Sacred Harp conventions in, 92, 110; as site of National Sacred Harp Convention, 273 (n. 5)

This entry would have been fine with a more general subhead, such as "Birmingham: . . . 92, 110, 273 (n. 5)." Finally, I might have reexamined the wording of some subheadings with the more refreshed energy and clearer mind that the editing stage can provide. For example, "Beecher, Lyman: interest in music reform of" would have sufficed with the subheading, "music reform of."

This lack of facility in editing the index was due not to my status as an author, of course, but to my inexperience as an indexer. I have since come to hold in reverent awe this unique process. Editing an index is not that difficult, and it can make dramatic improvements to an index.

DEMANDING TOO MUCH FROM THE USER

Another misconception I had was to assume that index structures are unambiguous, when in fact it is indexers who make them so. Even the most insightful entry, in fact, can be entirely undermined by ambiguity. The craft of indexing has everything to do with creating unambiguous information.

This process becomes second nature to experienced indexers, as a few examples from the *Public Worship* index illustrate. For instance, many headings had leftover undifferentiated locators in the main entry that should have been checked:

> Beecher: Lyman, 27, 29, 38, 42, 43, 271 (n. 13); and Connecticut Federalism, 15; and Dwight and "means of grace," 15, 18, 53, 61-62

The problem is in knowing what the undifferentiated locators represent: are they undifferentiated because they are of general importance, of too little importance, or is there is some other reason not to have a subheading?

Also, the relationship between the main heading and the subheading must be clear. If one forgoes syntactical marking (e.g., prepositions) in favor of a hierarchical relationship, the nature of the hierarchy may be unclear: "Sacred Harp writing: accumulative history, 150, 159-60." Do these passages concern the history of Sacred Harp writing or do they concern Sacred Harp writing that is historical in purpose and accumulative in style?

Another problem arose in packing subheadings with too much information. I found it difficult then (and still do now!) to "give up" (omit) information that seemed helpful and perhaps necessary. Sometimes the syntax made the meaning clear, and the result was merely distracting: "Beecher, Lyman: and Calvinist adversaries in Cincinnati, 58-59." Clearly, the significant phrase is "Calvinist adversaries," and one is only slightly wiser knowing where that happened.

There were other examples, however, where the relationship blurred: "Sacred Harp writing: rhetoric and culture, 166-70." There are three unexplained relationships here that the reader has no way to understand without looking at the text. While it is indeed difficult to compose a subheading that captures all these relationships, it is not difficult (though it is painful to an author) to give up the one that is less helpful to the user: "Sacred Harp writing: rhetorical features of, 166-170."

These troubles have much to do with underestimating the craft of indexing. They arise, I believe, from deeply held intuitions about what we believe we can presume when we communicate. I have found that good indexing entails a constant struggle against these intuitions.

"TOO CLOSE TO THE MATERIAL"

The affliction most often associated with author-indexers is their deep attachment to the subject matter. Wellisch (1991, p. 17) says that authors are "in most cases too close to their own work" and may either fail to index important facts or they index "every last trivial bit of information." Mulvany (1994, p. 21) quotes Wheatley Medal winner John A. Vickers, who says the author "should be the last person to index his own book, being too close to the text." Ironically, as I have discussed above, both recognize this also as a positive trait. So I want to explore a bit what makes this close knowledge both a curse and a blessing.

Looking back on the *Public Worship* index, I think I probably envisioned a kind of filing system for important information. Moreover, the significance of what I considered "information" was derived from the text. As an author, I held a good position to assess what on this basis was significant and what was not. The danger in this was that everything was important, leading to an index that grows without restraint—this is what is commonly called overindexing. My index had a 3.2 percent index-to-text ratio—adequate but modest by scholarly standards. Overall, I don't think I was susceptible to overindexing.

Rather, I have struggled with a different set of issues. Consider the following entry:

> Festivals: National Folk Festival, 113-14, 121, 123; White Top Folk Festival, 114; Fox Hollow Folk Festival, 191, 201, 281; Newport Folk Festival, 191; Oxford (Alabama) High School, 211-21; Kentuck (Northport, Alabama), 212; City Stages (Birmingham), 213; as secular events, 214

None of these particular festivals was posted separately. So, to find entries for the National Folk Festival, the reader must know to look under the broader term, "Festivals." This is an instance of what Wellisch calls "concealed classification" and what I have more recently heard described by the phrase, "Promote! Promote! Promote!" A user normally cannot be expected to know a classification scheme in advance.

More often, in fact, subheadings function as descriptors that cannot stand as main headings. The subheading "as secular events" is not a classifier, for example, and—given the way this subject is treated in the book—would not stand as a main heading. Moreover, where there are "classifier" type subheadings, there is sometimes neglected descriptive material that pertains strictly to that main heading. A more determined analysis of the pages indexed in the example above could yield the following:

> City Stages (Birmingham), 213
> Festivals: cultural pluralism and, 121; as music education, 113-14; national identity and, 123; role in Sacred Harp revival, 191; as secular events, 214; traditional singing and, 114, 211-13
> Fox Hollow Folk Festival, 191, 201, 281
> Kentuck (Northport, Alabama), 212
> National Folk Festival, 113-14, 121, 123

Newport Folk Festival, 191
Oxford (Alabama) High School Folk Festival, 211-21
White Top Folk Festival, 114

So the particular festivals in this entry should have been "promoted" from sub-headings to main entries where they belong. But, from the author's perspective, promoting results in a loss of information—of the implicit relations among the various festivals, of the indication of the importance of festivals as a whole, of the ability to easily scan for references to other festivals. These festivals probably should have been double-posted; short of that, however, their proper place was as main entries. More generally, an index is not primarily a classification device; rather, it is a collection of organized yet discrete entries into the text.

The reluctance to disperse information illustrated one theme of authorial overinvolvement; the other was overindulgence in the audience of informed readers. It is generally accepted that readers scan indexes in bookstores, looking for signs that the book relates to their interests. This is the circumstance of "naivety," where the reader does not know the book in advance, and the indexer has the obligation to anticipate it as an event with great potential. With my book, it was a consequence of operating too-close-to-the-text that I did not sufficiently prepare the book for this kind of encounter.

An obvious example was the omission of expected topics not necessarily suggested by the structure of the book. I had not included entries for "theology," "harmony," "Psalmody," "poetics," or "race" even though the book gave attentive treatment to these subjects. Although these terms were not suggested by the organization of the book, many readers would nonetheless expect to find them.

Familiarity with the subject was a particular hindrance in matters of place. In the festival list above, locations were given for the lesser-known events. But even informed readers shouldn't be expected to know the locations for all of the unidentified locales. Likewise the lengthy entry for Birmingham did not specify the locale—Alabama or England—for that city. Ordinarily, this logic should not be extended to suggest headings (such as "Alabama," with a collection of all locales in the state) that would mislead the reader into expecting a substantive discussion of the topic in the book.

Finally, there was a great temptation to index under the metatopic, in this case the term "Sacred Harp." I had the following main entries, each with numerous subheadings, in the index:

Sacred Harp conventions and singings
Sacred Harp minutes
Sacred Harp recordings
Sacred Harp revisions
Sacred Harp revival
Sacred Harp songs
Sacred Harp writing

This, no doubt, showed an authorial attachment to the metatopic—an overfamiliarity with stock phrases that seemed inseparable but would not have occurred to the naive reader. Additionally, there should have been cross-references to or from at least the following:

> conventions and singings
> minutes
> recordings
> writing practices

These oversights, as best I can tell, most likely arose from author bias. They were the consequence of seeing the material of the index internally, as an organizational device and not as an initial and freely motivated entry into the text. This does not mean that indexes cannot perform organizational functions. But to neglect the most naive occasions—where, for example, a reader looks for particular information not knowing if it is present or scans the index to assess the relevance of the book—is to sacrifice the essential purpose of the index.

AUTHORS AS COLLABORATORS

During my few years as a freelancer, I have had several occasions to index for authors. This circumstance commonly occurs in scholarly indexing since authors often are given the option to index their own book. If they choose not to do so, they most likely contract with professional indexers from a list provided by the publisher. Thus, the contractual scheme establishes the possibility of author-self-indexing at the outset, and the freelancer, to a degree, assumes the role of stand-in for the author.

The author has a much different stake in the index than the editor/publisher. The author's investment in the book is personal, having accumulated over many years of involvement with the subject matter of the book. Names that appear in the index are those of colleagues and friends. The particular approach the author brings to the subject may be thought to have important consequences for the field of study and for the author's career.

This personal investment is intensified by the economic circumstances of scholarly publishing. Unless a scholarly book enjoys widespread use as an undergraduate textbook, which is rare, author royalties amount to an inconsequential sum. Authors affiliated with universities will sometimes have their indexes funded by departmental accounts or grants. But some authors must pay for indexes out-of-pocket—and those who do may already have made drastic economic sacrifices to make time to write the book. In addition, if this is the author's first book, sacrifices may come in unanticipated increments, with the index as the least anticipated and the most tangibly financial.

Since I began freelancing, I have heard accounts suggesting that all of this presents an awkward situation for an indexer. Nonetheless, I have had very positive relations with authors. In every case, they have read my indexes carefully with an eye more to substance than style. Some have questioned my decisions or made suggestions for topics to add or emphasize more strongly. These queries are most always insightful and even stimulating, arising from the kind of thoughtful reading of the index that suggests respect for it.

Likewise, there can be little doubt that indexers provide authors with what may well be the most attentive reading their book will ever receive. A good index demonstrates a comprehensive and detailed understanding of the most complex issues in the book—an achievement that ranks among the author's chief ambitions in writing the book. I have learned to take much pleasure in my role as the book's most attentive reader, and I am certain this has had a positive effect on the quality of my indexes and of my relationships with author-clients.

FROM AUTHOR TO INDEXER

My author pedigree has had other consequences that have not always been positive. At times, empathy for authors has mutated into advocacy, and this has put me in awkward situations with editors and publishers. Having been employed by an author, I feel some duty to protect the author's interests. The most common issue is space limitation. If given a restriction, I always calculate the index-to-text ratio in advance—if it looks too small, I alert the project editor to my serious concern. On one occasion, a small press allotted two pages for a 120-page book. I knew they had a limited budget and were at the end of a signature, but I thought they could make a more conscientious effort to provide for an ample index in the book design. So I indexed a three-page sample as I would normally do, computed the number of entries that I would need to remove from the sample for the whole index to fit on two pages, and presented this gruesome scenario to the editor. This led to a broader discussion of redesigning the book, and the result allowed six pages for the index.

With larger scholarly presses, this would be more difficult or impossible. Project editors, moreover, do not ordinarily have the liberty to make such decisions on their own. *Public Worship, Private Faith* enjoyed ample space, but was subject to unconventional house specs. I knew, for example, that initial-uppercase main headings and page-ordered subheadings were, for very good reasons, not recommended by professional indexers. I made some grumblings, which had no consequence other than to put me in an adversarial relationship with the project editor. I have had to learn that even though with an author-client I might be employed by the author, it is actually the press that I need to nurture as a long-term client. On the whole, the lesson has been to temper author advocacy with good professional judgment.

Perhaps the most self-evident benefit of my author background has been its impact on marketing. Most of my first indexing jobs came through authors, even those who were provided indexer lists that did not include my name or who had previously employed other indexers. My social circles often put me in circumstances with other authors in various stages of writing. With little or no effort on my part, the subject of the index comes to the fore, implicitly or explicitly, including the possibly that I might do the work. Naturally, I have found it much more awkward to market my services to publishers, and imagine that indexers with publishing and editing background find the opposite to be true.

Learning the craft of indexing has entailed some unexpected lessons, one of which is the awareness of the consequences of the various paths to becoming an indexer. As an author, I have found some aspects of the indexing craft surprisingly unintuitive. On the other hand, my lengthy experience as an engaged, scholarly reader has been of inestimable value. I had anticipated that learning to index would be a mechanical process; instead, it has involved a dual effort of acquiring needed skills of the craft while at the same time learning the specific ways my experience would prove valuable.

REFERENCES

American Society of Indexers. 2001. "Authors and Indexes: Do It Yourself or Hire a Pro?" Pamphlet.

Bealle, John. 1997. *Public Worship, Private Faith: Sacred Harp and American Folksong.* Athens: University of Georgia Press.

Mulvany, Nancy L. 1994. *Indexing Books.* Chicago: University of Chicago Press.

Wellisch, Hans. 1991. *Indexing from A to Z.* Bronx, NY: H. W. Wilson.

———. 1992. "The Art of Indexing and Some Fallacies of Its Automation." *Logos: Journal of the World Book Community* 3(2): 69-76.

Chapter 9

The Quality of a Scholarly Index: A Contribution to the Discourse

© 2005 Margie Towery

The stage is brightly lit, ready for the game to begin. Three eager indexers provide their 10-second biographical sound bites. The categories on the board include Famous Indexers, History, Jargon, Tools and References, and Notable Indexes. *Jeopardy for Indexers* is about to begin!

"Tools and References for $100" starts the game. The answer is, "This is revised about every 10 years and published by a Midwestern university." One indexer gleefully punches the button: "What is *The Chicago Manual of Style?*"

"Jargon for $100!" The answer is, "These make readers dizzy." Buzz! "What are circular cross-references?" Eager to increase her dollar amount, the indexer says, "Jargon for $1,000." The answer is, "This includes conciseness, accuracy, reflexivity, consistency, and readability." The indexer answers, "What is quality?"

That is definitely the thousand-dollar question: What *is* quality? Indeed, it is a simple interrogatory with a complex and oft-debated answer—or answers. Certainly, it is understood differently, depending on the type of indexing being considered. If quality is indicated by certain characteristics, then we might agree that it may be different for a grade-school textbook compared with a scholarly monograph. Yet we must remember that not all scholarly books have scholarly indexes, or even any index at all.

Although other contexts may be noted here, this article focuses on quality in scholarly book indexes. This is not an article about basic rules of indexing. Further, the emphasis is on best-possible scenario indexing. In other words, most indexers recognize that in real-life, day-to-day indexing, they often face the challenge of time constraints and length limitations. Although I like to *think* that we give our best efforts in creating each and every index, I *know* that that's just not always possible. Thus, what follows is considered "quality" in a best-case scenario.

QUALITY, DEFINITIONS OF

Webster's Collegiate Dictionary (11th ed.) defines quality in several ways, with the following definition seemingly appropriate to the subject at hand: "an inherent feature; degree of excellence; superiority in kind; a distinguishing attribute." Although interesting, this is not particularly helpful in terms of specifics. So I consulted additional texts. Neither Nancy Mulvany's *Indexing Books* (indexed by Carolyn McGovern) nor Do Mi Stauber's *Facing the Text* (indexed by the author) includes an index entry for "quality."

The index for Hans Wellisch's *Indexing from A to Z* includes this entry:

> quality of indexes, 137
>   poor, 32, **54–56,** 269, 271, 419, 420

Page 137, which begins a section entitled "Depth of Indexing," leads with this: "The quality of an index can be evaluated by its depth of indexing which is the product of its exhaustivity and specificity." Well, yes . . . but that certainly does not go far enough, to my mind. Indeed, on pages 54–56 Wellisch lists 12 common mistakes that make a bad index, including such items as circular cross-references and misspelled names. We may assume that, given the bold page numbers in the index entry, these are his text's most important words on quality.

I wish to define quality in conceptual terms that weave together the more concrete and specific factors. *A quality scholarly index must be accurate, consistent, comprehensive, concise, readable, reflexive, audience-sensitive, and elegant.* Many factors underlie and connect each of these. Although I discuss many of these below, a mere article cannot pretend to be, well, comprehensive. Nonetheless, I offer this article as a contribution to the ongoing discourse about quality in indexes.

METATOPIC CONSIDERATIONS

In my experience, Do Mi Stauber has done more than any other indexer to highlight this issue. Her definition is succinct. The metatopic is "the structural center of the index: every single heading you create will be implicitly related to it" (Stauber 2004, p. 9). To that I would like to add my own cogitations on the metatopic of a book and its relation to quality.

I must point out that this serves as a point of discussion (i.e., disagreement) among indexers. Is it appropriate for the main subject (or subjects) of a book to appear as a main heading in the index? One argument replies negatively, insisting that if it is used, then the whole book would be indexed under it. While I don't disagree with this, *theoretically,* I would reply that most scholarly books are simply not so clear-cut. Indeed, I like to use the metatopic as a main heading because it is my "clue" to the reader as to the structure of the index as well as the scope of the text. That is, the metatopic main heading points the user to the ways in which the subject is covered in the text. I utilize two methods to do this (and no doubt other permutations exist as well). (An aside: The indexes for both Mulvany and Wellisch include lengthy entries under indexes, indexers, and indexing, the metatopics of their texts.)

The simplest way of using the metatopic main heading as a clue is to gather very few subentries under it and then use the cross-references as pointers to the main headings of most importance in the text (not necessarily, however, of most importance to the reader). For example, in Meredeth Turshen's *Privatizing Health Services in Africa,* health care is the metatopic. I included some subentries (e.g., access to) and then pointed to the "most important" main entries in the rest of the index:

> health care . . . *See also* drugs; hospitals; medical staff; primary health care; private health sector; public health sector

Moreover, cross-references must be accurate and consistent. A cross-reference that points to an entry for "public health sector" should send the reader to a main heading of "public health sector" and not one that reads "public health issues"—or worse still, "public health sector. *See* health care, public" (that old bugaboo of circular cross-references). Another more complex example of this technique comes from a book about science, technology, and medicine:

> medicine (subheads). *See also* body; essentialism; HIV/AIDS epidemic; prenatal diagnosis; psychiatry
> science (subheads). *See also* archeology; biology; developmental biology; feminist critiques; primatolog
> technology (subheads). *See also* computer science; consumption; engineering; history of technology; medical technology; prenatal diagnosis

A second way of using the metatopic as main heading works well when the book's subject is a more complex concept that is represented by a term with which readers may be unfamiliar. Thus, in Cynthia Enloe's *Curious Feminist,* the metatopic is "feminist curiosity." She utilizes this term in particular ways in relation to many subtopics in the book, such as militarization, globalization, and respectability. These are reflected in the subentries:

> feminist curiosity: . . . about globalization, 57; . . . about militarization processes, 220–31; . . . about respectability, 75–79

The page locators indicate the places in the text where she specifically applies the term. The subentries also point to topics that she considers in greater detail in the book. If we turn to "globalization," for example, the subentries read: "executives' construction of job market in, 45–46; feminist curiosity about, 57; of sneakers, 58–68; of U.S. cultural influence, 129, 186–87; women workers' priorities and, 63–64." That is, I use the metatopic (feminist curiosity) to point to only relatively limited instances of its application and yet the subentries point to topics (e.g., globalization) that are explored further.

I much prefer the first method because it is clearer to the reader. I envision readers wandering through their local bookstore, perusing books on a particular subject matter. Perhaps they flip to the index and look for that topic to see just how it might be covered in this author's text. Although indexers may be familiar with the discourse on metatopics and main headings, are readers aware of it? I wish I could think so, but I don't. So I want them to be able to find the main subject and then go from there to the rest of the index. In all fairness, though, I admit that this is my "take" on the reader's understanding of indexes. Some usability studies on how various audiences understand indexes and their structures would offer beneficial guidance for indexers.

ACCURACY

Accuracy seems like a "duh" factor. At a minimum, of course, page locators must be accurate. But this means more than just, "well-being, concept of, 12–14"—or creating a concordance in which every page for every term is listed. It also means that if "well-being" is discussed on page 12 and then the author turns to herbal supplements on the bottom of page 12 and onto page 13, then the page locators for "well-being" should more accurately read 12, 13–14. Or perhaps page 13 is made up entirely of a table that lists the various factors that well-being encompasses and the indexer has been instructed to use italicized locators for tables and figures. Then the entry should read "well-being, concept of, 12, *13,* 14," or, if there are other subheads as well, perhaps:

well-being: attitudes toward, 35; concept of, 12, 14; factors in, *13*

Then again, it would not be inaccurate to use simply: "well-being, 12, *13,* 14, 35." Thus, accuracy requires indexers to digest the textual content and create an index that mirrors that content.

Moreover, page numbers, in order to be accurate, must also be consistent, at least where possible. If a text discusses four countries and there are tables of statistics for each country, then the index should reflect (thus, be reflexive [another factor]) that:

Afghanistan: statistics on, *34*
Pakistan: statistics on, *98*

and so on. Thus, the accuracy of page locators includes preciseness of information and consistency in gathering and presenting that information.

It seems to me (and not everyone agrees with me on this) that accuracy and consistency dictate against what I call "floating page numbers." These are locators that follow a main entry, such as in the following example:

cats, 11, 34; caring for, 14–15; number of legs, 45–46; scent glands of, 56; tails of, 92

Pages 11 and 34 are floating page numbers. What do they mean, anyway? Are they the most important information? The least important? In my experience, most nonindexer readers have no clue as to what such locators indicate (nor do I!). It seems to me a disservice to readers (and to our larger concern for usability) to allow those page numbers to abide in that position. They are either important enough to warrant subentries or they're not, in which case, they should be deleted.

As with most indexing issues, there are exceptions. In some scholarly books and many trade and textbooks, a chunk of page numbers on a particular subject immediately follows the main entry:

yoga, 13–34
    hatha, 16 (and more subheads)

This is a reasonable practice that most readers seem to understand and that I view as more of a "lifeboat" of page numbers and less as floating detritus. On occasion I've also seen a single bold page number that indicates where the concept is defined. That makes sense to me as well. It is the random floating page numbers that really annoy me and leave me unclear as to what they mean.

One tactic that I've used when I felt the page numbers needed to be included but just couldn't legitimately come up with a subentry is using the term "mentioned." I've found this helpful particularly for people's names and sometimes have even forced it to sort to the end of the subentries (see more on passing mentions later in this chapter). My argument for including "mentioned" is that researchers interested in that person or concept may want to know even the tiniest details.

Accuracy should also be reflected in the choice of specific terminology. For example, in Enloe's *Curious Feminist,* I distinguished carefully between athletic footwear manufacturers and sneakers (sneakers being the author's preferred term, over athletic shoes). If there had only been a few page numbers, I might have unspecifically "smooshed" them together in both places. In this case, there were numerous subentries under each and cross-references. Specific manufacturers (e.g., Nike) were included as well.

Subentries must also be accurately worded. For example, I tend to distinguish between "as influence" and "influences on" (rather than using "influence of," which is fuzzier in its implications). On occasion, it's hard to construct a specific subentry, in which case accuracy trumps specific terminology. I may use "and" rather than pointing the reader in an erroneous direction (see more on connectors and prepositions below). In the following example, we can see that the two subentries have different meanings:

> mothers
>> of soldiers
>> soldiers and

As indexers, we are limited by what the text actually says, although we certainly apply our knowledge base in understanding the text and in creating a useful index. But sometimes I wish I could add an entry in an index that simply sends the reader to another, perhaps better, book on the subject!

CONSISTENCY

I can't emphasize enough the importance of consistency in an index, though of course there are times when inconsistency is useful (and even consistent). In terms of the latter, qualifiers come to mind immediately. By "qualifiers," I mean those parenthetical additions that clarify a main entry:

> Smith, Jane (Joe's mother)
> Smith, Jane (Joe's sister)

Most of the entries for people in indexes don't require such qualifiers but sometimes they are helpful to the reader. While it's inconsistent to use qualifiers for some and not others, it *is* consistent in that it provides the best information for the reader without cluttering up the index with unnecessary details (see more on audience, below).

Another point of consistent inconsistency may occur in a text that includes many place-names. Consider a book about California with asides about some little-known places in other states. I would probably not include qualifiers for the California place-names, but I would likely include them for non-California places:

> Bakersfield
> Deming (N.M.)
> San Diego

In this case, while not wishing to clutter the index with unnecessary qualifiers, it might be helpful to provide a comment on this in an introductory headnote. Indeed, a headnote is a useful tool, especially in explaining to readers about the structure of an index—or the consistent inconsistencies within it. In addition, in my personal quest to be helpful to readers, I almost always provide subentries for place-names. I argue that an entry for, say, San Diego, doesn't tell users much, but adding a subhead (e.g., climate of) lets them know immediately if it is of interest to them. I don't apply this argument to people, because I think that if someone is interested in a particular person, he or she will be willing to look up a few page numbers anyway.

When possible, main entries and subentries should be consistent in terminology. For example, if I use joint main entries, I want to use parallel construction:

> immigrants and immigration
> suffragists and suffrage (not the reverse)

Moreover, if such terms are discussed in the same fashion in the text (e.g., details about suffragists and immigrants as people rather than the concepts of suffrage and immigration), then they should both appear as such in the index. That is, the entries should be "immigrants" and "suffragists," not "immigrants" for one entry and "suffrage" for the other. I am not suggesting that indexers should impose a particular form of speech on every entry, rather that we adhere to the text and then utilize consistency and parallel construction *where possible*. Consider these subentries:

> Smith, Jane: career of; education of; sexuality of
> Doe, Joseph: education of; occupation of; sexuality of

Are Smith's career and Doe's occupation similarly considered? If so, then the same subentries should appear under each. This makes it easier for the reader to figure out what's what and to know where to look under a main entry, especially if there are lots of subentries under these people. Again, I am not suggesting that indexers impose consistency where it would change the author's meaning; certainly, career and occupation have different definitions and implications. Consistency is a factor that indexers must balance in aiming for quality.

The number of subentries and page locators is another point in which consistency is important. Consider a book in which many U.S. presidents are discussed on various pages throughout the text:

> Eisenhower, Dwight D., 66, 73, 78, 86, 92
> Johnson, Lyndon B., 34, 39, 52, 68, 99
> Kennedy, John F.: assassination of, 34, 56; election of, 67, 74; foreign policy of, 4

The author's favorite appears to be JFK. Is the above example consistent? Not to my mind. The entry for JFK does not require subentries anymore than the previous two. Thus, it behooves indexers to be consistent with the number of page locators allowed to stand without subentries. I generally pick a number of locators and use that throughout the index, particularly in terms of people. The number I use (5, 6, maybe even 8) depends on the structure of the index (are people central or peripheral to the text?) and on the length of the index (in a longer index, I am more willing to allow a bit longer string of page numbers). [An aside here: how do you count the number of page locators? I've had this discussion with other indexers and have found that I am in the minority in terms of how I count locators. Here's an example: 4, 87–89, 101. Would you say that is three locators? Or five?? I argue the latter is the correct number. Here's another example, just for hyperbole: 4, 87–99, 101. How many locators are there? Just three? I say there are a lot more than three.]

Another issue of consistency is balanced treatment when pulling entries from the text. Consider a book on science education. In a chapter on curriculum components, one section includes a paragraph about creationism and a paragraph about evolutionism. There are at least two and probably three entries: one for curriculum, one for creationism, and one for evolutionism. Regardless of your feelings about this subject, balanced treatment should be given to similar comments. That is, when concepts are discussed in a similar manner, they should be indexed in a similar manner.

Finally, "connectors" and prepositions should be used consistently. Scholarly indexes require such connectors (see more on this in the section on readability, page 91). Words such as "and," "of," "versus," and "as" should be used consistently in constructing subentries (and they are part of the parallel construction issue). Moreover, while indexers disagree on whether it is best to place "and" at the beginning or end of a subentry, they generally agree that it should be consistently placed throughout an index:

> railroads: fruit production and; lumber industry and
> fruit production: railroads and (*not* and railroads)

COMPREHENSIVENESS

As an indexer who focuses on scholarly books, I think the thing I most struggle with is the issue of over- versus under-indexing—and being consistent in the depth of indexing throughout a lengthy (maybe less-than-interesting—or less interesting in some parts than others) text. But these three concepts (depth, exhaustivity, and specificity) are critical to a quality scholarly index.

Let's return to Wellisch's *Indexing A to Z* for a moment. He writes that depth is the "product" of "exhaustivity and specificity" (p. 137). Further, "exhaustivity refers to the extent to which concepts and topics are made retrievable by means of index terms" (p. 175); and "specificity refers to the extent to which a concept of topic in a document is identified by a precise term in the hierarchy of its genus-species relations" (p. 439).

How do these concepts apply to creating a scholarly index? I doubt that anyone would argue with this: scholarly books are indexed more intensively (i.e., in more depth) than trade books and some textbooks. Moreover, the terminology is often more complex (with a need for greater specificity) in scholarly books (on the other hand, terminology in some scholarly books is hopelessly muddled). Thus, a quality scholarly index should present a more exhaustive, deeper level of indexing, with a concomitant specificity of terminology.

I struggle with this issue because of my tendency to index heavily rather than lightly. That is, I tend toward more exhaustive indexing (in more ways than one!). Another way to examine this is to figure out what constitutes a (mere) passing mention as compared with substantive information. That's more easily said than done, for me, with my heavy, exhaustive indexing style. Information that I might consider substantive, another indexer might call a passing mention. In scholarly books, though, I feel justified in indexing the possibly marginal because it may be far more than marginal to some readers. I bend over backward in mentions of people, in particular (though not always) because I think someone might remember a discussion point and a mentioned person in association with that point.

Interestingly (for me, anyway), I have after a decade of indexing modified my indexing practice in a way that means I struggle less with this complex issue than previously. I had long been an indexer who sat down in front of the computer with the page proofs in front of me and read and created entries all at once. That is, I didn't preread, and the only premarking I did was to indicate page ranges for text subheadings. While working on an encyclopedia project in early 2004, I found that I could not work this way. Faced with three columns of tiny print and sometimes the need for what felt like a hundred entries per page, my eyes (bifocals and all) simply failed. I couldn't keep track of where I was in a column, let alone on a page! So for that project, I read and marked at my dining room table (which overlooks a wooded ravine), then changed my venue to the office and computer for keyboarding the entries. I discovered three things: I liked not being in front of the computer all of my work time (and I liked having woods and a ravine to peruse at times); I made fewer entries and found it easier to balance between over- and under-indexing; and I could spend less time editing, because in effect, I'd already edited twice (once while I read and marked and a second time as I typed entries). I would never argue that everyone should apply this technique, because people process information in different ways (e.g., some of us are aural learners, some visual). I would suggest that we keep our processes (and brains) open to different ways of creating indexes.

CONCISENESS

As indexers this is one of our most important goals: presenting an organized structure in as concise a manner as possible while at the same time maintaining clarity and comprehensiveness. That sounds like double-talk, but I like to think of all of these factors in quality as puzzle pieces. Indeed, there are times when I have sacrificed specificity for conciseness. On occasion, in the editing process I may come across two main entries that have only one or two subentries. When it will still be clear to the reader, I may decide to combine them (e.g., the above joint main entries of "immigrants and immigration"). As long as the meaning remains clear, I feel that losing a bit of the specific terminology is acceptable and more concise— also less reading improves usability for the audience.

In the entry stage of index creation, I tend to create longer main entries and subentries than I will retain in the final edit. Allowing myself a bit of wordiness to begin with means I can work toward conciseness in the editing stage while also holding onto the intended meaning. In addition, conciseness must often be balanced against an alphabetical sort for the subentries. That is something to always keep in mind in editing an index.

Cross-references may help or hinder the conciseness of an index. Theoretically, I suppose, we should not need cross-references. Everything should be entered in full wherever it should be, as many places as necessary, right? Of course, in that case, the index could grow to a lengthy part of the book. Certainly, many readers complain about cross-references: "I looked up X only to have to turn back to B," they grumble. I like cross-references. But then, I like puzzles, map reading, and mysteries, too. Nonetheless, cross-references, *if used succinctly and with care,* lead readers to specific information as well as give them clues to additional entries they may wish to check (and clues to the structure of the index, as discussed above).

At this point, I would like to focus briefly on the clumping versus spreading issue. Anne Leach introduced this idea to me (and others) early in my indexing career and I have found it most helpful. Consider a book that discusses cultural differences in hairstyles, hair ornaments, and hair coverings, with approximately nine subentries under each, such that double-posting is not desirable. Should the main entries be spread?

coverings, hair
coverings, leg
hair styles
ornaments, hair
ornaments, leg

Or should the entries be clumped?

hair coverings
hair ornaments
hair styles
leg coverings
leg ornaments

Regardless of clumping or spreading, of course, cross-references can direct the reader, one way or the other. But I think it may indeed be more efficient for the reader to have the entries clumped. Certainly, within an index, the entries should, I think, be either consistently clumped or consistently spread—that facilitates retrieval—and once again we see the benefit of consistency in an index.

In another example, from Adrian Johns's *Nature of the Book,* there were many entries for manuscripts, copyright issues, astronomy and science, printing, and people, such as Isaac Newton. Following is my application of clumping to the batch of printing-related concepts, each of which has subentries:

> print. *See also* history of printing
> print culture
> printers. *See also* apprentices; stationers
> printing. *See also* history of printing
> printing houses
> printing press. *See also* steam press; type; typography
> printing revolution

I used clumping for other related concepts as well. This was a long index (44 printed pages), and I present it here to show how clumping facilitates retrieval.

READABILITY

In the pursuit of conciseness and even consistency, a quality scholarly index should not jettison one of the essential characteristics that, in some ways, separates it from, say, a textbook index: that is, readability. (Don't get me wrong, I know many textbooks are just as complex as "scholarly" books! Here I am referring to straightforward textbooks. At least in my admittedly limited experience with textbooks, I have found them less "readable.")

An editor once told me that she understood what the book was about after reading my index to it. While some would argue that that index probably had too much information in it, I would suggest that it nonetheless succeeded in being both comprehensive and readable. What does it mean for an index to be readable? A quality scholarly index is called upon to make clear the obscure or even confused text, to simplify complex concepts, and to translate jargon whether of new or old origin, and to do all of this in a fashion that flows into an identifiable structure that in turn serves to get readers to the information they seek.

Cross-references, both *see* and *see also,* play a critical role. I often tell authors who are reviewing an index I've written for them: Read the index through quickly the first time, paying attention only to main entries and cross-references, because this allows them to see the structure of the index. Then I suggest they read it through more carefully, looking this time at the subentries. (I do this now because I once had an author, after reviewing the first half of a 90-page index, say, "Oh, I get it! I see what you've done!" But he refused to go back and reverse his changes, which of course affected the entire structure. I doubt he would have followed my advice even if I'd given it.)

The connectors and prepositions I mentioned above are also critical. They are the tiny pieces that explain the connections between the main entry and the subentry. Consider the following examples in which those small words make a big difference (my preference is in parentheses):

> readers: influence (influences on); interpretation (interpretation by)
> reading: history (history of); labor (as labor)
> regulation of the press: attitudes (attitudes toward); printers (printers and)

Notice I tend to put the "and" at the end of the subentry. I might mention that I avoid having too many inversions in subentries (e.g., reading: as labor, considerations of). It just seems to take longer to wrap the brain cells around them; on the other hand, the more complex a book is, the more difficult it is to keep the index simple, concise, and readable.

Clumping entries, described above, also fosters readability. Finally, format makes a difference in readability. Because most scholarly book indexes are printed in a run-in format, the index is limited to one level of subentry. But we can "tweak" that format in different ways. One of my favorites is the modified run-in format. I found this particularly helpful in *Art and the Crisis of Marriage: Edward Hopper and Georgia O'Keeffe,* by Vivien Green Fryd. The text explores Hopper's and O'Keeffe's marriages and their and their spouses' artwork. Using the modified run-in format, I broke the entries under each of these four people down into the following (parallel construction here, too):

> artistic elements
> career
> exhibitions
> life
> works

There were of course sub-subentries under each of these. In general I prefer the printed format to start each of these on a new line preceded by an em dash, with the sub-subentries run-in from there. In this case, the compositor ran the whole batch together but set the subentries (above) in bold. (I wish I could believe space was an issue, but there are four lovely blank pages at the end of the index.) Nonetheless, I argue that a modified run-in format can be helpful in fostering readability, an essential component of quality scholarly indexes.

REFLEXIVITY

A quality index should reflect the text from whence it emerges, that is, it should be reflexive. The index that the editor reviewed (and found it helped her understand what the book was about, mentioned above) was reflexive of the book. It provided a sense of the book for those who might fully read the index (yes, I know, only editors and indexers ever actually read a whole index).

Webster's Collegiate Dictionary defines reflexive as "directed or turned back on itself; . . . marked by, or capable of reflection; . . . of, relating to, characterized by, or being a relation that exists between an entity and itself," and so on. And that is exactly how an index should be reflexive of the text. That does not mean that it directly repeats it. A common mistake of beginning indexers is to regurgitate the text in the index rather than consider and reflect the text in useful entries.

Should the author's biases also be reflected in the index? Here is another oft-debated question we indexers like to discuss, and there are no firm answers, at least in my opinion. If I were indexing a book in which an author used racist language, I might very well try to find a way to reflect *but not repeat* that language in the index. If I had a sense that a book was going to be truly offensive, I might not accept the project when offered. But most of us accept projects based on schedule and topics, not knowing if there is going to be something egregiously awful in it. So I guess I would opt for allowing the author's bias to shine through, but I might request that my name not appear in the book as indexer, if I seriously wanted to disassociate myself from a particular cause.

One of the ways in which I try to reflect the text is by using my intuition as well as my rationale in understanding it. I tend to think that intuitive processes allow the art of indexing to come into play, if you will. It's also helpful in thinking about new approaches to indexing a concept or term, about treatment of a really jargon-filled text, and about pushing myself away from trying to fit information into my tried and true subentries (e.g., background of; definition of; influences on; so-and-so's relationship with). In addition, I apply my intuition to thinking about possible audiences.

AUDIENCE

As indexers we often talk about creating indexes with the interests of the possible audiences in mind. Moreover, we think we know what various readers or users of a given book will want to find. Most of the time, we're probably as much on target as is possible. But we also sometimes forget to move away from our indexer-based perceptions of audiences. Indeed, I suspect that we often attribute far more savvy to index users than they really possess. I suppose that's one reason that I think that pointers (cross-references), qualifiers, and headnotes are useful tools (although, to be honest, I can't say *I* turn to the beginning of an index and see if there's a headnote before I try to look something up). We can also interpret jargon

94

for index users, as far as is possible. And we can cross-reference or double-post acronyms and their spelled-out versions.

Certainly, we do our best but we truly have a shortage of data on what index users really want. What we need is usability testing of our indexes on the targeted audience. Even if it were deflating, usability testing would provide us with much needed information.

ELEGANCE

Ah, this is an elusive, but integral, characteristic of a quality scholarly index. How might we define elegance in an index? We'll begin with *Webster's* again: "refined *grace* or dignified propriety; . . . tasteful *richness of design* or ornamentation; . . . dignified gracefulness or restrained beauty of style; . . . scientific *precision, neatness, and simplicity*" (italics added). Thus, the idea of elegance gathers much of what we've been discussing above: restraint and ornamentation, precision and richness, simplicity and neatness. Indeed, elegance is a balance of art and science that includes concrete measurables and hard-to-define immeasurables.

Elegance shines through in many ways: in structure, conciseness, comprehensiveness, readability, in the language itself—in all the factors that make up a quality scholarly index. It helps to have an elegantly written text to index, of course. That makes the achievement of elegance easier, I think. But can we create an elegant index from a mediocre text? In some cases, yes; in other cases, no. Sometimes the best we can hope to do is to create some semblance of order in an index to a disorderly book. Sometimes, though, the elegance comes through in an index in which we've worked through much of what we've just discussed. And then we know we've created a quality scholarly index.

REFERENCES

Enloe, Cynthia. 2004. *The Curious Feminist: Searching for Women in a New Age of Empire.* Berkeley: University of California Press.

Fryd, Vivien Green. 2003. *Art and the Crisis of Marriage: Edward Hopper and Georgia O'Keeffe.* Chicago: University of Chicago Press.

Johns, Adrian. 1998. *The Nature of the Book: Print and Knowledge in the Making.* Chicago: University of Chicago Press.

Mulvany, Nancy C. 1994. *Indexing Books.* Chicago: University of Chicago Press.

Stauber, Do Mi. 2004. *Facing the Text: Content and Structure in Book Indexing.* Eugene, OR: Cedar Row Press.

Turshen, Meredeth. 1999. *Privatizing Health Services in Africa.* New Brunswick, NJ: Rutgers University Press.

Wellisch, Hans H. 1996. *Indexing from A to Z.* 2d ed. New York: H. W. Wilson.

Index

Carolyn Sherayko

Consistency in indexing
cross-references, 83, 91
legal indexing, 19, 23
names, 11, 12, 33
quality and, 86–88, 91
titles, 8, 55
Criticism, works of, 5–6
Cross-references
accuracy/consistency of, 83
acronyms, 94
alphabetic variations, 19
case names, 21
conciseness and, 90–91
editing of, 73
names, 12, 32, 54–55
readability and, 91–92
relationships, 49
synonyms, 48–49
titles, 9–10
Cyrillic script, 57–58

D

Delivery of index, 35–36
Derrida, Jacques, 39
Diacritics, 53–54
Discipline-based knowledge
economics, 47
languages, 58–59, 61–65
law, 15, 28
music, 2, 4, 5, 6, 71–72
philosophy, 46
political science/public affairs, 31
Double-posting
acronyms, 33, 34, 94
case names, 35
editing of, 73
legal indexes, 26
names, 32

E

Economics, 47–52
background knowledge for, 47

equations/figures/tables in, 51
index structure in, 49–51
references for, 47–48
terminology in, 48–49
Editing of indexes
importance of, 72–73
law, 26, 28
quality and, 90
Editors
delivery of indexes to, 35
indexer-client relationship and, xii,
79
index exhaustivity and, 6, 51
queries to, 32, 36
revised/supplemented texts and,
24–25
space limitations from, 78
style guidelines from, 35, 51, 78–79
Electronic products, legal, 27–28
Elegance of index, 94
Encyclopedias
See also Reference works
legal indexing, 25–26
Endnotes, indexability of, 34
Equations, 51
Exhaustivity, 6, 51, 88–89
Exhaustivity of index, 6, 51, 88–89

F

Figures, 51
Finance. See Economics
Finding indexing work, 28
Footnotes, indexability of, 34
Foreign languages, 53–68
background knowledge for, 58–59,
61–65
diacritics, 53–54
initial articles in, 55
music, 3, 9–10
philosophy, 38, 56
procedures for approaching, 65–66
references for, 66, 68

Personal names. *See* Names, personal
  and corporate
Phenomenology, 39–40
Philosophy
  arguments in, 40–41
  background knowledge for, 46
  foreign languages in, 38, 56
  of music, 6
  references for, 39, 41–46
  terminology in, 6, 37–40
Place names
  qualifiers for, 76, 86
  subentries for, 87
Political economy. *See* Economics
Political science
  background knowledge for, 31
  index consistency/structure, 33–34
  names in, 32–34
  references for, 31–32
Postmodernism/poststructuralism,
  39–40
Preposition use. *See* Connectors and
  prepositions in subentries
Pseudonyms, 12
Public affairs. *See* Political science

Q

Qualifiers, 7–9, 86, 93
Quality of index, 81–94
  accuracy, 84–86
  audience considerations, 93–94
  comprehensiveness, 88–89
  conciseness, 89–91
  consistency, 86–88, 91
  elegance, 94
  exhaustivity, 88–89
  metatopic considerations, 82–84
  readability, 91–92
  reflexivity, 84, 93
Queries to authors/editors, 32, 36

R

Readability of index, 91–92
Redlines, working from, 24–25
Reference works, indexing of
  legal. *See* Legal indexing
  music, 6
Reference works as resources
  See also Internet resources
  economics, 47–48
  foreign languages, 66
  law, 29–30
  music, 12–13
  philosophy, 41–44
  public affairs, 31–32
Reflexivity of index, 84, 93
Regulations (law), 17–20
Revision of index, 24–25, 29
Run-in format, subentries in, 5, 35, 92
Russian language, 56–58

S

Sartre, Jean-Paul, 39–40
Selection of terms. *See* Term selection
Sorting. *See* Alphabetization
Space limitations in indexes, 26, 78
Spreading, of entries, 90–91
Statutory law, 17–20
Stauber, Do Mi, 23, 82
Structure of index
  economics, 49–51
  foreign language texts, 57–58
  law, 22, 26, 28–29
  metatopics in, 83–84
  music, 74
  political science/public affairs,
    33–34
Style guidelines for indexes, 32, 35,
  51, 78–79
Subentries
  in biographies, 4–5
  classified lists and, 10–11, 75–76
  in complex indexes, 23, 49

Subentries (*cont.*)
  connectors and prepositions in, 26,
      86, 88, 92
  editing of, 73
  governmental agencies, 33–34
  "mentioned," as useful, 85, 89
  names, 4–5, 87, 92
  order of, 7, 71, 78
  place names, 87
  readability of, 92
  in run-in format, 5, 35, 92
  specialized law topics as, 18
  wording of, 26, 35, 51, 74, 85–86
Synonyms, 48–49

T

Table of cases, 20–21
Tables, 51
Terminology
  See also Names, personal and cor-
      porate
  economics, 48–49
  foreign languages, xii, 3, 38, 55–56
  historical, 3–4
  jargon, 37–38, 91, 93–94
  law, 15, 18, 25
  music, 1–4, 6
  philosophy, 6, 37–40
  political science/public affairs, 34
  subject-specific meanings of, 4, 18,
      37–38
Term selection
  accuracy of, 85
  balanced treatment in, 88
  clumping vs. spreading and, 90–91
  consistency in, 87
  contexts for, 33, 48, 76
  foreign language immersion and,
      66–67

  indexable pages and, 34
  legal, 29
  specificity of, 88–89
Textbooks
  depth of indexing in, 89
  foreign language, 56–58
  law, 16–17
Theory and criticism, works of, 5–6
Titles
  consistency and, 8, 55
  cross-references from, 9–10, 21
  initial articles in, 55
  laws and case names, 18, 20–21, 35
  music, 6–10
Trade books, 89
Translation. *See* Foreign languages
Transliteration, 38, 57
Treatises, legal, 21–22

U

Usability studies, need for, 84, 94

V

Vickers, John A., 75

W

Web sites. *See* Internet resources
Wellisch, Hans
  on authors as indexers, 69, 70–71,
      75
  on classified lists, 75
  on comprehensiveness, 88
  metatopic entries in, 83
  on names, 55
  on quality of indexes, 82

Z

Zafran, Enid, 17, 21

More Great Books
for Indexing Professionals

Genealogy and Indexing
Edited by Kathleen Spaltro

Indexes are the essential search tool for genealogists, and this timely book fills a conspicuous void in the literature. Kathleen Spaltro and contributors take an in-depth look at the relationship between indexing and genealogy and explain how genealogical indexes are constructed. They offer practical advice to indexers who work with genealogical documents as well as genealogists who want to create their own indexes. Noeline Bridge's chapter on names will quickly become the definitive reference for trying to resolve questions on variants, surname changes, and foreign designations. Other chapters discuss software, form and entry, the need for standards, and the development of after-market indexes.

Softbound • ISBN 1-57387-163-X

ASI Members $25.00 • Non-Members $31.25

Software for Indexing
Edited by Sandi Schroeder

In this thorough and objective review of the software products used in indexing, professional indexers share their favorite features, tips, and techniques. Starting with a chapter on dedicated indexing programs, CINDEX, MACREX, SKY Index, and wINDEX are compared. Coverage of embedding software includes Framemaker, Microsoft Word, PageMaker, QuarkXPress, Ixgen, Index Tool Professional, and IndeXTension. For those interested in online and Web indexing, HTML/Prep, HTML Indexer, and RoboHelp are all covered. Other chapters discuss database software, customized software that works with dedicated programs, and automatic and machine-aided indexing.

Softbound • ISBN 1-57387-166-4

ASI Members $28.00 • Nonmembers $35.00

Indexing Specialties: Medicine
Edited by L. Pilar Wyman

This in-depth look at the indexing specialty field of medicine is the latest in the popular series from ASI and Information Today, Inc. With contributions from over a dozen noted medical indexers, the book features 13 chapters in four parts: "Medical Indexers" includes an interview with two veteran book indexers and a biography of a database indexer; "Medical Indexes" includes examination of award-winning medical indexes and medical index reviews; "Medical Indexing" gets into the heart of the matter and provides detailed discussion of indexing medical specialties, with chapters on indexing food and nutrition, nursing, and general medicine, and three chapters on database indexing; and "Resources" lists guides to medical reference tools and Internet-based resources.

Softbound • ISBN 1-57387-082-X

ASI Members $28.00 • Non-Members $35.00

Indexing Specialties: Law

Edited by Peter Kendrick and Enid L. Zafran

This release in the popular "Indexing Specialties" series is devoted to the topic of legal indexing, with contributions from more than a dozen leading practitioners. Part 1, "Getting Started," provides practical advice for new legal indexers and those considering a career in this challenging field. Part 2 covers the ins and outs of "Indexing and Tabling Legal Cases." Maryann Corbett addresses "The Unique Challenges of Indexing Statutory Materials" in Part 3. Part 4 offers a critical assessment of "New Technologies and Methodologies," and the book concludes with Part 5, "Reflections on Legal Indexing," which includes "must-read" chapters by Dorothy Thomas and Kate Mertes. Editors Kendrick and Zafran have created a unique and valuable reference that belongs on the desk of every legal indexer.

Softbound • ISBN 1-57387-113-3

ASI Members $28.00 • Non-Members $35.00

Indexing Specialties: History

Edited by Margie Towery

This compilation of articles focuses on the indexing of history textbooks, art history, medieval and Renaissance history, Latin American history, and gender and sexual orientation language issues. The authors' intelligent advice and discussions will assist both new and experienced indexers who work in the field of history and related disciplines.

Softbound • ISBN 1-57387-055-2

ASI Members $12 • Non-Members $18

Indexing Specialties: Psychology

Edited by Becky Hornyak

Continuing the series that addresses specialized areas for indexers, Becky Hornyak has assembled a panel of experts that includes Sandy Topping, Carolyn Weaver, and Carol Schoun. The emphasis is on indexing textbooks and books aimed at clinical practitioners in the field of psychology. Includes extensive, annotated listings of print and other resources for psychology indexers.

Softbound • ISBN 1-57387-149-4

ASI Members $20.00 • Non-Members $25.00
